The Essence of Reiki

The Definitive Guide to Usui Reiki

First published by O Books, 2008
O Books is an imprint of John Hunt Publishing Ltd., The Bothy, Deershot Lodge, Park Lane, Ropley,
Hants, SO24 0BE, UK
office1@o-books.net
www.o-books.net

Distribution in:

UK and Europe
Orca Book Services
orders@orcabookservices.co.uk
Tel: 01202 665432 Fax: 01202 666219
Int. code (44)

USA and Canada
NBN
custserv@nbnbooks.com
Tel: 1 800 462 6420 Fax: 1 800 338 4550

Australia and New Zealand
Brumby Books
sales@brumbybooks.com.au
Tel: 61 3 9761 5535 Fax: 61 3 9761 7095

Far East (offices in Singapore, Thailand,
Hong Kong, Taiwan)
Pansing Distribution Pte Ltd
kemal@pansing.com
Tel: 65 6319 9939 Fax: 65 6462 5761

South Africa
Alternative Books
altbook@peterhyde.co.za
Tel: 021 555 4027 Fax: 021 447 1430

Text copyright Andy Chrysostomou
and Dawn Mellowship 2008

Design: Stuart Davies

ISBN: 978 1 84694 099 6

Printed by Chris Fowler International
www.chrisfowler.com

O Books operates a distinctive and ethical publishing philosophy in
all areas of its business, from its global network of authors to
production and worldwide distribution.
This book is produced on FSC certified stock, within ISO14001
standards. The printer plants sufficient trees each year through
the Woodland Trust to absorb the level of emitted carbon
in its production.

The Essence of Reiki

The Definitive Guide to Usui Reiki

Andy Chrysostomou
and
Dawn Mellowship

BOOKS

Winchester, UK
Washington, USA

CONTENTS

DISCLAIMER

The information contained in this book is for reference purposes only. Reiki is a traditional energy based healing method and is a complementary therapy. Reiki is not a medical or clinical practice and should not be used as a replacement for medical treatment. In case of injury or illness you should always consult a qualified medical practitioner of your choice.

Preface

Life is really incredibly simple. Only humans have the ability to make life difficult. Mikao Usui found a way to heal directly, to heal any condition, no matter how serious. This was a gift given to him by God, to share with the world and now the world will see in this book for the first time, the real Way of Usui. Take the time to understand this book with objectivity and an open mind. Don't let the words of your teachers' rule your way of thinking. Look to your higher self, look to God and you will see that all the answers you could ever need await your action. To doubt these answers is to doubt your own existence. Take steps towards God, fulfil your higher paths and practice the only true system of what has come to be known as 'Reiki'. Practice the Usui Method of Spiritual Energy Healing. This is all you will ever need...the secret of inviting happiness, the miraculous medicine of all diseases.

Dawn Mellowship

Introduction

Between us, we have been practicing and teaching Reiki for a number of years. Through our Reiki work, much research and many hours of daily self-healing, we have developed a deep understanding of Usui Reiki Ryoho, i.e. The Usui Method of Spiritual Energy Healing, more commonly known in the West as Reiki. We have looked at books written by so-called and often esteemed Reiki 'experts' and come across many members of the Reiki community as part of our work.

There are some fairly good Reiki books that are well researched and give lots of historical information about Reiki, but in many there seems to be a writer's interpretation, which in some cases distorts or even changes the real meaning of the information. It very quickly came to our attention that there is a distinct lack of knowledge and understanding about how Reiki really works and how to utilise the energy in the most effective way.

With this book we are sharing what we know to be true about Reiki, because through our work, we have seen how effective Reiki really can be when used properly. What we want to do with this book is to get across the beauty and the true essence of Usui Reiki Ryoho. Only by understanding the essence of Reiki can we truly embody the way of life that is Reiki.

Throughout this book we have used both our own knowledge and the guidance of Usui-sensei. We use the title Sensei as a term of respect for the founder of Reiki. Sensei means honourable teacher and is a title given by students for their teacher, whether it is martial arts, Reiki, or any other discipline.

Our aim is to continue Usui-sensei's work and to take Reiki to the next level, in the way Usui-sensei originally intended. This book may challenge existing views widely held about Reiki, and cause some Reiki healers to question their practice, and some Reiki teachers to question their teaching.

We are not expecting people to blindly follow anyone's words, including ours; a book should always be read with a discerning eye. All we ask is for people to have an open mind, trust their intuition and try working with the Reiki energy the way Usui-sensei intended it to be used. Try working with the Reiki energy as we describe and see the difference it makes to your healing work, both for yourself and for others. You may be pleasantly amazed at what you can achieve. As Usui-sensei said, "Reiki is the miraculous medicine of all diseases," and the "Secret method of gaining happiness."

SECTION ONE
ABOUT REIKI

Chapter One

What Reiki is

What Exactly Is Reiki?

Reiki is an energy-based healing and self-development system that originated in Japan. This is pretty much the standard, practical description of Reiki. It is accurate in so far as Reiki works with channelled naturally occurring energy for healing purposes and for self-development, but it falls short of actually telling you enough about what Reiki really is. Reiki is so much more than this. Reiki is the possibility of enlightenment, of complete fulfilment and inner contentment, the answer to all your questions. To learn Reiki, and to be attuned or connected directly to the source of this astonishing energy is truly life changing. Having a profound connection to this loving and nurturing energy is the most amazing blessing.

Some people choose to call this energy the Universe, some the Divine, some the Creative Energy, some call it God, some simply see it as an intelligent and loving energy and others as natural energy that exists all around us. It makes no difference how you define or describe the source of the energy; words only get in the way of what this energy truly is. It is both an individual experience and an intrinsically personal relationship between the source of the energy and the Reiki practitioner, which develops and grows over time.

Reiki is a fascinating journey of self-discovery and growth that starts with the attunements and continues through self-healing. As awareness raises and understanding increases so too does happiness and fulfilment. Reiki is an empowering healing gift that absolutely anyone can possess and use to treat themselves and others for any and every condition. Reiki can bring about the most profound of changes to any and every student that chooses to learn and practice it. Reiki really is a gift from the Universe.

Reiki The Word

To define the system of Reiki we need to first define the word Reiki. Reiki is a Japanese word made up of two kanji 'Rei' and 'Ki'. Kanji originate from China and are written characters, which can be either pictorial or phonetic in nature. Both kanji have various interpretations and we have only included the ones that are relevant to Usui Reiki Ryoho:

Rei- (*Literal Japanese - spiritual or sacred*) Rei energy makes up one of the energies used in Reiki. Usui-sensei described this energy as "light coming from the hand" and it is used to treat the spirit or soul. Generally in the West, this has come to be accepted as Universal Energy, which exists everywhere around us, outside all living things and some say, inside all living things. Other generally accepted interpretations of Rei energy are the highest spiritual consciousness, spiritual healing energy, naturally occurring electromagnetic energy and God's highest power. However this term is interpreted it does not change what Rei actually is, a form of electromagnetic energy with a high frequency.

Ki- (*Literal Japanese - energy*) Generally, Ki is used in the context of life force energy, which exists inside all living things and surrounds all living things. This energy is the other component energy of Reiki. Ki energy has a lower frequency range than Rei energy.

Ki, as believed in many Eastern traditions, needs to flow freely throughout the body. If we have an emotional trauma or a physical illness or injury a blockage is created and the flow of Ki is disrupted.

Conversely, if a blockage occurs in our body, this will disturb the path of the energy through our bodies and we then develop an illness. To promote good health our Ki needs to be strong and able to flow freely. The healthier we are, the more Ki we will have flowing through our body.

The actual word Reiki is used to describe spiritual healing in Japan (amongst other interpretations). There are many other systems of hands-on spiritual healing that were known as Reiki in Japan both before and after Usui-sensei developed the Usui System of Natural Healing, known as Usui Reiki Ryoho (*Lit. Japanese – Usui spiritual energy healing method*). The teachings of Usui-sensei were also known as Usui-do, meaning 'the way of Usui' and the actual hands-on healing was known as Usui Teate.

As the popularity of Reiki increases so too does the number of different forms or styles of Reiki. There are over 140 different types of Reiki practiced around the world now, and this number continues to grow. Some of these new Reiki systems were developed from Usui-sensei's work and others have no relation or connection to his work whatsoever, but have latched onto the title Reiki.

Throughout this book we will use the terms Reiki or Reiki Ryoho or Usui Reiki Ryoho to describe the teachings and methods of Usui-sensei. We are not referring to any of the many other types of Reiki in existence.

Reiki The System

In very simple terms, Reiki is a natural healing system that uses naturally occurring variable frequency energy to work on any condition. Reiki does not require any medical knowledge nor any special gift or ability, and it does not involve massage or manipulation.

The energy used in Reiki is electromagnetic in nature yet feels nurturing and loving and can work on any level, physical, emotional, mental and spiritual. Reiki is more than just a connection to this amazing energy. Reiki is more than a spiritual growth and healing method. It is the embodiment of the spiritual enlightenment Usui-sensei achieved after many years of hard work, study, and self-development.

What Usui-sensei managed to do with his Reiki Ryoho was distil his life's work and knowledge into a single, simple spiritual method, that reconnects anyone to the source of the energy and allows them achieve a connection with their true spiritual nature and follow their higher path to enlightenment.

We cannot overstate the importance of Reiki. It brings the possibility of spiritual growth and enlightenment within the grasp of every individual on Earth, regardless of their age, position, knowledge, awareness, spiritual beliefs, faith or religion.

Reiki in its original form consists of a set of teachings with distinct levels and sub-levels (similar to Japanese martial arts). Each level includes specific techniques and knowledge that must be mastered before moving onto the next level.

Within each main level there are a variety of sub levels with specific requirements of both practice and knowledge, which also need to be mastered before moving on. As in martial arts, students are assessed at each level and have to demonstrate the required ability before they are awarded the grade for the level.

Over the years Usui-sensei modified and simplified his Reiki Ryoho to make it easier to learn and more accessible to ordinary people.

Reiki is a complete and self-contained system, which includes many methods and techniques as well as a great deal of information and knowledge. The system of Reiki requires of its practitioners hard work and effort, commitment and dedication. Reiki is not something you undertake lightly or on a whim or fancy. Reiki is not a label or badge to wear to show how 'new age' or spiritual you are. Reiki is a way of living your life in a conscious and guided way, for the higher good of yourself and others. Being attuned by a competent Reiki teacher and following a Reiki path can be one of the most amazing and life changing experiences you can have on Earth.

The Usui Method of Spiritual Energy Healing was developed as a means of self-development and growth, as a path to enlightenment, as well as a healing method. The core philosophy underpinning Reiki is the Japanese concept of 'oneness', of uniting Heaven and Earth, Man and God. In effect what this means is that we are all, both physical and spiritual, human and Divine. We can, if we choose to, live our lives in a more spiritually guided way by connecting to our Divine nature within ourselves, which is a part of the creative Divine energy.

This is the core purpose of Reiki. To achieve this state of 'oneness' we need to heal and then connect our three energy bodies, our physical, our emotional and our spiritual. These bodies are healed using the different energies of Reiki. Healing the physical, the emotional and the spiritual bodies is the basis of Reiki. Once we have healed these three bodies sufficiently, we can create 'oneness' within ourselves. We then need to create the 'oneness' with the Divine or God or the Universe.

This tradition of healing the physical, emotional and spiritual bodies is very different to the more modern Western Reiki concept of chakra healing. Reiki is not based on the Indian chakra system, as is now commonly believed, although many Western Reiki teachers do include chakra healing in their Reiki courses. The confusion probably stems from the hand positions taught by Mrs Takata that appear to be based around the main chakras, whereas in fact the hand positions actually work on the head and throat area and the main organs and systems of the body for overall healing.

Chapter Two

The Reiki History

There are various stories and theories regarding the history of Reiki, both the history of Mikao Usui (Usui-sensei) and the ancient origins of Reiki.

The only factual information we have is the written documentation of Usui-sensei himself and the knowledge passed down from his original masters. The primary source of documented history about Usui-sensei can be found carved on his memorial stone at his gravesite in Tokyo, which was placed there by his students in 1927, a year following his death. Much of the documented information and knowledge handed down over the years has been contained within the Usui Reiki Ryoho Gakkai (*Lit. Japanese – Usui Spiritual Healing Method Society*), but hopefully this knowledge will eventually be shared with the rest of the world.

Origins Of Reiki

There are many theories about the history of Reiki such as: it is an ancient Tibetan healing art; it is the way Jesus healed; it is a lost Buddhist healing art; it originated in India; it originated in ancient Egypt, and so on. Many Reiki teachers suggest that Usui-sensei only re-discovered Reiki, but in his own words, Usui-sensei said, "My Usui Reiki Ryoho is an original, there is nothing like this in the world." Usui Reiki Ryoho was founded by Usui-sensei and is not a lost tradition or ancient art, nor did Usui-sensei learn or copy his Reiki Ryoho from anyone else. He said "I've never been given this method by anybody nor studied to get psychic power to heal." It is quite obvious from his words that Usui-sensei considers himself the originator of his Reiki Ryoho.

Obviously, there are now, and there always have been, many forms of hands-on healing. There have always been and always will be natural healers that can put their hands on people and make them feel better and even cure them of illnesses and injuries, but they are not practicing Reiki. Reiki is a system of energy healing that was discovered and then developed by Usui-sensei over a number of years into an effective, yet simple, method of healing and spiritual growth.

Usui Reiki Ryoho

Usui-sensei practiced and taught hands-on energy healing before his enlightenment on Mount Kurama. He taught many students his hands-on healing system for many years and was a well-respected teacher.

His methods for healing changed once he was enlightened with the knowledge of his Reiki Ryoho. This new method itself changed over time as Usui-sensei developed and refined the method and as he gained deeper understanding and greater awareness. This method for healing has been known as the Usui System of Spiritual Energy Healing, Usui-do (the way of Usui), Usui-Teate (the application of Usui-do), Usui Reiki Ryoho and simply as Usui Reiki or Reiki.

With this new method Usui-sensei was able to heal by connecting to and using external energy. Usui-sensei was now able to treat any condition whether it was physical, emotional or spiritual by using the relevant frequency energy. This was achieved through the use of the relevant shirushi (symbol) and its corresponding jumon (name) or kotodama (mantra).

One of the key elements of this new method of healing was that students could be re-connected or have their connection enhanced to the source of the energy by the formal, ritualised process of attunement or empowerment carried out by the teacher or master.

Usui-sensei originally taught Reiki in the manner of his martial arts teaching. Students would come for training on a regular and frequent basis, and would be taught techniques that they would practice repeatedly until they became proficient. Once a student reached the required level of proficiency they would be awarded that particular grade and then move on to practice for the next grade. Students would receive Reiju (empowerment) as part of every class they attended to help raise their frequency and thus their spiritual development and healing ability.

The Gokai (*Lit. Japanese - five precepts*) were recited at each class and were a focus point for meditation. Keeping to the Gokai i.e. following the Reiki precepts was a major part of Usui-sensei's teaching. Students would have to keep to the Gokai in their daily lives as well as becoming proficient in all the required techniques to progress on their Reiki path. For Usui-sensei 'right thinking' and 'right living' were an essential part of Reiki. Only through 'right thinking and right living' with regular self-healing is the necessary self-development and spiritual growth possible that can lead students to happiness and enlightenment.

Students were taught and practiced intuitive methods for healing, such as Byosen Reikan Ho & Reiji Ho. For some students these methods proved difficult to master, so Usui-sensei with Dr Hayashi developed the Ryoho Shishon (*Lit. Japanese - healing method guide*), which gives hand positions for specific illnesses. Students would use these hand positions until they had developed sufficiently to work intuitively.

The Reiki shirushi (symbols) and their corresponding jumon (name) and kotodama (mantra) were added to the teachings in 1923 to enhance the connection to the energy achieved through Hatsu Rei Ho and the other meditations.

For some of Usui-sensei's students, this type of regular on-going training was impractical, so the later attunement process was used in place of the older Reiju to enable students to study Reiki and reach the required levels in shorter timescales. For example, Dr

Hayashi taught level 1 and 2 (Shoden & Okuden) as five two-hour modules over five consecutive days. This was the method Usui-sensei used when teaching some of the Japanese Naval Officers and the students he taught on his travels around Japan, as well as his later students at his Tokyo school. This is generally the way Reiki is taught now.

Mikao Usui

Mikao Usui or Usui-sensei as he was known by his students, was born in the first year of the Keio period (known as Keio Gunnen) 1865 on the 15th August in Taniai village in the Yamagata district of the Gifu Prefecture in Japan.[1] He was born and raised as a Tendai Buddhist, but he also followed the Japanese religion of Shintoism.

His first name is Mikao, and his given name is Gyoho, his forefathers were named Tsunetane Chiba or possibly Toshitane Chiba[2] (there is some doubt as to which it was) and his mother's family were Kawai. His father's name was Taneuji, with the given name of Uzaemon.[1] The Chiba clan were at one time a wealthy and influential Samurai family. Usui-sensei's family were Hatamoto Samurai, the highest level within the samurai ranks. During the Tokugawa shogunate the Hatamoto were the upper vassals of the shogun.

Usui-sensei was born into a time of great change in Japan. The Meiji Emperor ended Japan's isolation from the rest of the world and introduced sweeping social change at every level of Japanese society. The change began in earnest with the opening of Japan's ports in 1865, though this was a change forced upon them by the United States through the threat of war and invasion, rather than a desire for contact by the Japanese themselves.

With the introduction of Westerners and their culture and influence, Japanese society was bound to change. The Meiji Emperor introduced laws to disband the Samurai class and in 1871 they were ordered to cut off their topknots and put aside their swords.

Many of the Samurai were integrated into the civil service, but their once privileged and powerful military status was resigned to the history books. This was a difficult time for the once proud Samurai families and for some it was a time of humiliation and dishonour. There followed a period of protest and unrest, but eventually the change was accepted, albeit grudgingly.

Usui-sensei had two brothers called, Sanya and Kuniji and a sister called Tsuru.[2] As a child, Usui-sensei was bright and intelligent with a real thirst for knowledge. By the age of twelve he had started learning martial arts, something that was not only common, but expected for male children of Samurai families. His love of martial arts continued throughout his life.

He is known to have worked very diligently with his studies; on his memorial stone it states that, "he surpassed his peers in hard work and endeavour." It goes on to state that his love of knowledge and reading extended to Christianity, Buddhism, Taoism, medicine, psychology, kiko, mysticism, and the psychic and spiritual arts.

Kiko is a Japanese form of Qigong, a healing discipline that teaches the practitioner to develop their Ki (life-force energy) for their own self-development and well-being and for healing purposes. The practitioner builds up their Ki (life force energy) through specific stances, breathing and movements, which clears any blockages within their body to allow the free unhindered flow of Ki. This built up Ki can also be used to heal others, but by doing this it is depleted and has to be continually developed and strengthened by the practitioner.

Usui-sensei devoted his entire life to studying and self-development. He travelled widely around Japan and he visited Europe and it is said he visited the USA. He studied in China to further his knowledge, which was not uncommon at the time. For a period of time he worked as a private secretary to Shinpei Goto, a politician who went on to become the mayor of Tokyo in 1920.

Usui-sensei was married to Sadako Suzuki and they had two children, a son called Fuji and a daughter called Toshiko.

Mikao Usui's Discovery Of Reiki

Usui-sensei was known as a man of virtue and a man of Great Spirit, because he worked tirelessly through meditation and study to improve body, mind and spirit.[1]

Such a man that uses this Great Spirit to do collective good and teach knowledge for social purposes is known as a sensei or teacher, a man of merit.[1] This is a term of respect and is used by students when referring to their teacher.

Usui-sensei was an incredibly warm, gentle, caring and compassionate man. He was a strong but humble man, always remembered with a beaming smile on his face.

Usui-sensei used his discovery of Reiki to help as many people as he could. He kept his Reiki simple, natural and therefore easy to learn. He envisioned the Great Reiki of the Universe spread throughout the world in order to bring about healing, not only to individuals, but also to societies and the Earth as a whole.

Usui-sensei was a truly great and enlightened man. He started a system of healing that is spreading love and light throughout the world. He was intelligent and hard working and he overcame many difficulties throughout his life. He practiced meditation and martial arts and applied himself to the task of improving and strengthening mind, body and spirit with the aim of becoming a better person.

Long before his satori (*Lit. Japanese – spiritual awakening or enlightenment*) on Mount Kurama, he was well known and well respected as a healer. He practiced and taught both martial arts and healing. He was an enlightened and spiritual man who gave his time and knowledge widely and freely to further the cause of an improved society. He believed that, "right thinking and right living" were essential to self-development and spiritual growth.

The other essential element to any kind of spiritual growth is having a strong connection to the Great Reiki of the Universe, a connection to the source of the energy, to God, the Creative Energy, or whatever term you choose to use. This connection can be fostered in a number of ways, through meditation, prayer, chanting, fasting, and we are sure there are other ways also.

The way Usui-sensei taught his students to gain this connection altered throughout his life, as his methods evolved and developed. His teachings eventually became his Reiki Ryoho, the Usui Method of Spiritual Energy Healing. This method of connection and subsequent healing combined with 'right thinking and right living' is the key to spiritual growth and enlightenment that Usui-sensei has bequeathed to the world.

In his quest for self-development, Usui-sensei travelled to Mt Kurama (*Japanese Kurama Yama*), where he undertook a twenty-one day retreat called Kushu-Shinren (*Lit. – Japanese painful discipline-difficult training*), which is a form of Shyu Gyo (*Lit. – Japanese training or discipline*).[1] For the twenty-one days Usui-sensei prayed, chanted, meditated and fasted by abstaining from any food. It is believed he undertook this particular Shyu Gyo in March 1922.[2] It was on the twenty-first day of this Shyu Gyo that Usui-sensei received his satori and the knowledge of his Spiritual Healing Method, his Reiki Ryoho. There are other texts that allude to the teachings of Usui-sensei being decades old by the time he formed the Usui Reiki Ryoho Gakkai, though it is believed these teachings were earlier forms of healing that he eventually developed into his Reiki Ryoho after his satori.

On his memorial stone it is described as, "after 21 days of a severe discipline without eating, he (Usui-sensei) suddenly felt One Great Reiki over his head and attained enlightenment and he obtained Reiki Ryoho." In his own words Usui-sensei says he, "felt an electricity around his head". He was spiritually awakened and given the knowledge of the Reiki Cure.

Usui-sensei used this Reiki of the Universe to heal himself and his family. The healing effects were immediate, so Usui-sensei wanted to share Reiki Ryoho with other people. Usui-sensei initially worked helping the poor of Kyoto.

In April of the eleventh year of the Taisho period, 1922 Usui-sensei opened his new dojo (*Lit. Japanese – place of the way, i.e. a place of learning*) in Aoyama Harajuku, Tokyo. This was open to the public for both healing and teaching. Usui-sensei was said to have started the Usui Reiki Ryoho Gakkai (*Lit. Japanese – Society Of The Usui Spiritual Energy Healing Method*) at the same time.

This society still exists today and keeps the teachings and written records of Usui-sensei within its membership. This society is not open to foreigners, nor are the members allowed to share any of the knowledge with non-members, although one member, a Reiki teacher called Hiroshi Doi, was given permission to share certain information with Western Reiki practitioners and teachers. Additionally, some Reiki teachers have managed to meet with and get information from some of the surviving students of Usui-sensei, though some of these students only studied Usui-sensei's older, pre-Reiki Ryoho teachings.

People came from around Japan to receive treatment and to learn Reiki Ryoho from Usui-sensei. His students state on his memorial stone that, "many pairs of shoes of visitors from near and far were lined up even outside of his dojo."

In September of the twelfth year of the Taisho period, 1923, the great Kanto earthquake hit Tokyo and Yokohama. There was massive loss of life and suffering through the earthquake and resulting fires. The suffering was incredibly overwhelming, and Usui-sensei went out every day to treat as many people as he could. On his memorial stone his students' stated that he "cured and saved an innumerable number of people."

Demand for Reiki increased to such an extent that in February of the fourteenth year of the Taisho period, 1925 Usui-sensei had to build a bigger dojo in Nakano, Tokyo. His reputation spread throughout Japan and he travelled across Japan giving healing and teaching.

Usui-sensei taught more than 2000 students and 16 of these reached the top of his teachings to become masters or teachers. Some have said the number of teachers was 21, but this figure may include students that studied with Usui-sensei before his discovery of his Reiki Ryoho.

Usui-sensei called his Reiki Ryoho the "secret method to invite happiness" and the "miraculous method to cure all diseases." The Gokai or Reiki precepts were included in the teachings to help develop a pure and sound mind. Usui Reiki Ryoho is a way of living that allowed one to become healed on all levels in order to gain enlightenment.

Usui-sensei died on 9th March, of the fifteenth year of the Taisho period, 1926 of a stroke while in Fukuyama.[1]

After the death of Usui-sensei, some of his students and masters/teachers stayed within the Usui Reiki Ryoho Gakkai and carried on with Usui-sensei's work. The society became secretive and closed. Only members were allowed the knowledge of Usui Reiki Ryoho. Membership is still by invitation only and foreigners are not allowed membership.

The rest of the masters/teachers left the Usui Reiki Ryoho Gakkai and some started their own schools to teach hands-on healing, in some cases with some variation to the teachings of Usui-sensei. The first form of Usui Reiki Ryoho that was brought over to the West was from the lineage of Dr Chujiro Hayashi.

There are a number of forms of Reiki practiced in Japan, which originate with Usui-sensei's teachings. Some of these forms of Reiki are now taught in the West, as Western Reiki teachers have trained in Japan and brought the teachings back with them.

How close these teachings are to Usui-sensei's Reiki Ryoho is open to question. Students will have studied with Usui-sensei at different times and at different stages of the development of his Reiki Ryoho. Thus they will have their own recollections and understanding of the system and its methods, and therefore will be teaching Reiki Ryoho as they remember it. The later students will perhaps be teaching Reiki in its more developed form, the form more closely resembling that taught by Dr Hayashi. Over the years since Usui-sensei's death much of his knowledge has unfortunately been lost and much has been changed. For the discerning Reiki student there are now many areas of research and much good knowledge available, along with a great deal of very confusing, irrelevant and poorly understood information. We can all improve our knowledge and therefore our understanding and practice of traditional Usui Reiki Ryoho should we wish to. It may take a great deal of research, time and patience, but it is worth the effort.

Dr Chujiro Hayashi

Dr Chujiro Hayashi (or Hayashi-sensei) was born in Tokyo on 15th September 1880. Dr Hayashi was married to Chie and had two children, a son called Tadayoshi and a daughter called Kiyoe.[2]

When he started learning Reiki Ryoho with Usui-sensei in 1925 he was a retired officer of the Japanese navy and a member of the navy reserve. He was a medical doctor and surgeon. He studied with Usui-sensei for around ten months before Usui-sensei's death in 1926. He managed to reach the top level of Usui-sensei's teachings in that time and became a master/teacher. He remained within the Usui Reiki Ryoho Gakkai until 1931, when he left to open his own clinic and school in Tokyo called the Hayashi Reiki Kenkyu Kai[2] (*Lit. Japanese – Hayashi Spiritual Energy Research Society*).

Dr Hayashi saw Usui Reiki Ryoho in terms of its healing potential, whereas Usui-sensei saw his Reiki Ryoho more as a way of living a better life, a spiritual path that would lead to happiness, fulfilment and ultimately enlightenment. Dr Hayashi was tasked by Usui-sensei to develop and expand the practice of his Reiki Ryoho into a much more clinical form of healing. Together they developed the Reiki Ryoho Hikkei (*Lit. Japanese – Spiritual Energy Healing Method Handbook*). This was given to all students and is still given to members of the Usui Reiki Ryoho Gakkai to this day. By this stage Usui-sensei's Reiki Ryoho teachings had developed and evolved into a three level format, shoden (*Lit. Japanese – first level teachings*), okuden (*Lit. Japanese – second level teachings*) and shinpiden (*Lit. Japanese – mystery teachings*).

Dr Hayashi kept treatment records for his patients and had printed Reiki class manuals, similar to the Reiki Ryoho Hikkei, for his students.

Initially Dr Hayashi taught the three levels of Usui Reiki Ryoho with a gap in between each level and the students would work as volunteer healers at his clinic for a prescribed number of hours each week before moving onto the next level. Later on Dr Hayashi taught the first two levels shoden and okuden as one course over five days as five two hour modules.

Dr Hayashi taught Usui Reiki Ryoho in line with Usui-sensei's later teachings, that is, with the shirushi (symbols) and their jumon (name) and kotodama (mantra). He also attuned students with the shirushi and their jumon and kotodama as opposed to the earlier method of Reiju, which did not generally use these elements.

He is said to have charged surprisingly high fees for his courses, which is perhaps why Mrs Takata followed his example with her fee structure.

Dr Hayashi died on the 10th May 1940. It is said by Mrs Takata that he died of a self-induced stroke, whereas one of his students has stated that he died by "breaking an artery." Others have suggested that as a military man he would have committed ritual suicide or seppuku with a short-sword. Whatever method he used, Dr Hayashi committed suicide because as a naval officer he would have been expected to participate in the impending war with the United States and he preferred to take his own life in an honourable way, rather than bringing dishonour and shame to himself and his family by refusing to do his duty as an officer of the

Imperial Navy.

This only serves to demonstrate that even those with little interest in spirituality when they first receive Reiki denju (*Lit. Japanese – initiation*) will change through the use of Usui Reiki Ryoho as they heal themselves and connect to their true spiritual nature.

Dr Hayashi had taught a total of 13 masters/teachers by the time of his death, one of them being Hawayo Takata. Mrs Takata brought Usui Reiki Ryoho over to the West in the 1930's.

Mrs Hawayo Takata

Mrs Hawayo Takata was a Japanese immigrant living in Hawaii. She was born on 24th December, 1900 to Mr and Mrs Otogoro Kawamura. She was named Hawayo after their new homeland of Hawaii. Her father worked on a sugar cane plantation as a cutter. Hawayo worked as part of the sugar cane plantation owner's household. She eventually rose through the ranks to become head housekeeper.[2]

It was while working in this household that she met her future husband, Saichi Takata, the plantation bookkeeper. They were married and had two daughters.

Unfortunately her husband died in October 1930 at the age of 34, leaving her to support her two children. Life became extremely hard for Mrs Takata, and after five years she became physically and emotionally ill. Soon after, she travelled to Japan to inform her parents of the death of one of her sister's and to receive treatment for her illnesses.

Whilst in Japan, she attended hospital and was diagnosed with asthma, gallstones, appendicitis and a tumour. Mrs Takata was due to have surgery but she sensed it was not necessary (she says she heard a voice telling her not to have surgery). Rather than opting for surgery, she asked at the hospital if there was an alternative treatment she could have. She was referred to Dr Hayashi's Reiki clinic by the hospital dietician.

Mrs Takata received healing from two practitioners daily, over a period of four months, (six months has also been quoted) after which she recovered fully. She was so impressed with the Reiki treatment, she asked to learn, but initially Dr Hayashi refused because she was a foreigner. Eventually, after demonstrating her commitment to Reiki and volunteering at his clinic, Dr Hayashi relented and taught her Reiki level 1 (shoden) and level 2 (okuden) over a period of time. It was 1937 when Mrs Takata finally graduated to the second level (okuden).

In 1937 Mrs Takata returned to Hawaii to start her own clinic in Honolulu. Dr Hayashi and his daughter followed a few weeks later to help set up her clinic. They stayed with Mrs Takata for around six months, at the end of which Dr Hayashi gave her the rank of master/teacher.

In 1938, Mrs Takata became the thirteenth and last master/teacher to be initiated by Dr Hayashi.

Mrs Takata spent the rest of her life sharing Reiki. She set up several Reiki clinics in Hawaii for healing and teaching.

She is known to have charged fees for her treatments, and in the case of those unable to afford these fees she treated them for free. She was a very practical healer, looking at lifestyle issues that could benefit her clients, as well as giving them Reiki treatments. She was interested in nutrition and gave dietary advice to clients to aid their recovery.

Hawayo Takata travelled around Hawaii giving healing and it is said, teaching, but there seems to be little evidence of her teaching during her years in Hawaii.

She stayed in Hawaii until the 1970's when she moved to mainland USA and it was here that she started offering Reiki courses. She only taught level 1 and level 2 until 1976, when she started teaching Reiki Masters.

Mrs Takata made certain changes to the Reiki she was taught by Dr Hayashi, perhaps to make it more acceptable to western society.

She adapted Usui-sensei's teachings to suit the political situation created by World War II. Much of the spirituality and intuitiveness was removed, leaving a practical, Westernised system of healing, which was in effect much simpler, easier and quicker to learn. Mrs Takata made some false claims to promote Reiki in the USA, such as: Usui-sensei had taught at a Christian University (Doshisha University) in Japan; Usui-sensei had studied at Chicago University. She claimed Usui-sensei was a Christian and at one point claimed that Reiki had Tibetan influences (because Tibetan culture was popular at the time). She also claimed in her publicity material that she was the only living Reiki Master in the world.

Mrs Takata allowed students to take her Reiki courses without any prescribed time gap between levels. This is more in line with the Japanese way of teaching, where students progress when they are ready to move on. She would not allow students to take notes or keep copies of the symbols and she did not give class manuals. She introduced a $10,000 fee for Reiki level 3, and insisted the masters she initiated swear an oath to teach Reiki exactly as she had done. The $10,000 fee for the level 3 course was possibly due to the high fees Dr Hayashi charged and was likely to reflect the price she would have paid for her training.

Mrs Takata initiated 22 Masters before her death in 1980. These 22 masters went on to teach Reiki, some in the way of Mrs Takata, as with the Reiki Alliance, and some in their own ways with new forms of Reiki. One reason why Reiki teaching fragmented after Mrs Takata's death was the fact that she taught Reiki classes without giving the students manuals and would not allow students to take notes. The 22 masters she taught all had different recollections from their training and so could not agree a basic form for the teaching of Reiki.

This is basically how Reiki initially came to the West. The vast majority of Western Reiki practitioners have a lineage that goes back in some way to Usui-sensei via Mrs Takata. Now there are many other branches of Japanese Reiki that have been brought to the West, with different lineages back to Usui-sensei and with perhaps different teachings. It is doubtful Reiki would be as popular or even known in the West if it was not for Mrs Takata.

Chapter Three

Why We Need Reiki

Usui-sensei believed that society was in need of both healing and improvement, and one way to make society better was to heal and develop individuals within society. That was true in the early 20th century, and it is true now. Usui-sensei taught his students to live their lives with "right thinking and right living" for their own self-development and to honour his Reiki Ryoho. We need Reiki as much, if not more now than in Usui-sensei's day, even with all our medical and technological advances. We still have a need for a natural healing system, which we can use as individuals to help ourselves to not only heal but to grow and develop emotionally and spiritually.

In practical terms, Reiki can be used to treat physical injuries and illnesses, emotional traumas and conditions and ultimately to heal the soul. On a purely physical level, Reiki allows us to treat our own illnesses and injuries as a stand-alone therapy and where necessary as a complement to medical treatments. Being able to assist in our own healing process is both empowering and liberating. With Reiki we can unobtrusively treat emotional traumas, no matter how major or how old and forgotten they may be. Having the ability to deal with emotional traumas and everyday stresses and worries in a healthy way means we can avoid the negative thought patterns that can lead to illness. With Reiki we can initiate and strengthen the repair and regeneration processes for ourselves, and in time get to a state of wellness and health that we can maintain with regular self-treatments and a healthy lifestyle.

Everyone longs for happiness, health and fulfilment, generally through material success and emotional attachments. We all have our own ideas of what we think we need to achieve these goals, yet many of us continue to be unhappy and unfulfilled, even if we achieve the material success and relationships we crave. The single fundamental and essential goal that many of us fail to recognise is the attainment of our spiritual growth. The one thing above all else that can lead to true happiness and fulfilment is the one thing we have forgotten about.

Perhaps if spiritual growth could be manufactured, advertised, endorsed by celebrities and sold at extortionate prices, we would all be lining the aisles to purchase some. Unfortunately, spiritual growth is seen by many as 'new age rubbish', irrelevant to us in this time of ever increasing material wealth and technological and scientific advances.

But, if we really think about where we are as a global society, how far have we come in the last 2000 years? Have we learned to resolve conflict without violence and war? Have we learned to love each other unconditionally? Have we learned to share our wealth with those of greater need? Are our lives richer and happier? Are we any more fulfilled? Are we any wiser? We think not. So what have we really achieved with all our advances? We still have wars, we still have millions living in abject poverty, we still have millions starving and we still have unnecessary suffering inflicted on individuals as well as on entire societies.

We live our lives as a daily struggle trying to satisfy our physical wants and emotional desires, unknowingly creating an imbalance in our spiritual nature and disconnecting from our higher selves. We are persistently damaging ourselves, and some of us will even happily inflict harm on other people without a thought or a care. The only way to improve society is to improve each individual in that society. This is one of the main reasons Usui-sensei wanted Reiki to be shared with as many people as possible.

Emotional and spiritual imbalances can manifest in our lives in many ways. We are sure we have all, at some point in our lives, felt

some of the following:
- a deep sadness and lack of fulfilment
- feelings of being lost and directionless
- a lack of meaning and purpose to our lives
- feeling like we are simply 'going through the motions' rather than living life
- low self-worth and feelings of inadequacy
- feeling alone even when around other people
- that there must be more to life than this

...the list goes on.

All or some, or indeed any of these negative feelings can even manifest as physical or emotional illnesses over a period of time.

So what is the answer? The most basic answer is to connect to our true spiritual nature and live our lives in a conscious way. We need to always be aware of our thoughts and our actions, as these will have consequences for ourselves and for those around us. We always need to think and act for the higher good rather than our own selfish desires. In Usui-sensei's words, we need to live our lives with "right thinking and right living." Sounds really simple right? Well, in our materialistic and self-centred society, with all the pressures of life, some we cannot avoid, others we choose to take on, it can be incredibly difficult to do this.

Once you are attuned to Reiki you will feel a growing connection to your true spiritual nature, your higher self, which will start to guide you through life. Your higher self is your connection to the source of the energy, whether you call that source God or the Universe or any other term is of no consequence, language is irrelevant.

Once this connection is established by the attunement process, you then have the opportunity to develop this connection, making it stronger and taking yourself closer to the source of the energy. This you do by self-healing regularly and by living your life in the right way for your higher path. This is, in fact, how you grow and develop spiritually.

As a means of spiritual growth, Reiki is one of the simplest and most effective methods we have *ever* come across. But Reiki has so much more to offer. Reiki is a complete method for healing the mind, body and soul. Reiki can be used to heal the physical body, the emotional body and the spiritual body by channelling energy at the relevant frequency for each. Healing on these three levels creates a balance, unity and oneness with the Universe.

This is what Usui-sensei meant by gaining happiness. Reiki helps you to detach from your everyday existence and see the 'bigger picture' instead of living inside a box that disconnects you from everyone and everything in the Universe.

Chapter Four

The Benefits of Reiki

Where do we begin? Reiki can heal you on every level. The Reiki of the Universe is infinite and limitless in its potential. Reiki can be used to treat any physical condition, by using the frequency of energy required by that condition, and it can clear energetic blockages allowing the body to heal itself.

Reiki is a wonderful spiritual path, if you choose to pursue this direction, and it re-connects you to the source of the energy or God or the Universe, enabling you to self-heal whenever you feel the need. By self-healing daily you are ensuring that you are balanced physically, emotionally and spiritually. You are also devoting some much needed time to yourself and fostering your own awareness, transporting you further along your higher path. You will become far more intuitive, allowing you to make healthier decisions in life and feel a wonderful sense of 'completeness.'

It is now recognised that stress plays a huge factor in every area of our daily lives, contributing to a range of both physical and emotional illnesses. The Health and Safety Executive have reported that up to five million people in the UK alone feel "extremely" or "very" stressed by their work and more and more people are finding that the fast paced lives they tend to lead cause a huge strain on their health and well-being.

Reiki has a positively calming effect, filling you with a sense of inner peace and serenity that will ensure that stress does not control your life. Reiki allows you to detach yourself from your everyday existence, seeing situations more as an objective outsider, rather than being helplessly embroiled in events that you feel are beyond your control. By learning or experiencing Reiki you will gain a real sense of self-purpose and inner clarity that may have eluded you previously.

These busy lifestyles we lead not only cause stress they can also take a huge toll physically on our bodies. Through continual physical self-healing you can not only prevent the onset of illness, you can use Reiki directly on physical injuries and illnesses ranging from mild back pain to major illnesses and injuries. Whatever the illness or condition is, Reiki can always help. Some students who learn Reiki never suffer from the coughs, colds and other niggling illnesses that plague so many people, because they are constantly self-healing.

One of the most amazing things about Reiki is that, unlike other energy healing therapies, Reiki allows you to heal on every level. There is no one on this Earth who has not experienced emotional traumas in their life. These traumas hold you back, stalling your self-development and preventing you from being your true self. They cause you to create an image of yourself, based around what you think other people or society expects and wants from you.

Whilst all this is going on, your higher self, the real you beneath the facade, is being neglected and desperately trying to grab your attention. By using Reiki on yourself you can remove the energy attached to all the traumas you have experienced, so you will no longer feel any pain associated with those events. Once this has been achieved you are finally free to be yourself, not what you think you should be or what you think others would like you to be.

We can often feel that our lives lack direction and that no matter what we do, we just cannot seem to pinpoint exactly what would make us happy. The only thing that can really ever make you truly happy is fulfilling your purpose for being on Earth. Reiki re-connects you with your true purpose opening your eyes to a whole new world and way of living that you had previously missed out on. This leaves you feeling far more focused about where you need to be directing your precious resources and time.

Many people spend years or even their entire lifetimes feeling that they are in the wrong jobs, wrong relationships or wrong situations. Reiki opens up your mind to the things that you really need in life, rather than the things you thought you wanted. There is nothing quite so liberating as acceptance and learning to want the things you need, rather than the things you were never meant to have. Letting go to the will of the Universe is a fundamental prerequisite to attaining inner peace.

Learning Reiki is not only a wonderful tool for self-development and healing, Reiki enables you to heal others, either purely on a voluntary basis or as a registered working Reiki practitioner. Society has become quite individualistic and many people feel that they are taking so much from life and would like to give something worthwhile back. By learning Reiki up to level 2 you have the wonderful gift of being able to heal those around you that need your help. Sharing your gift of healing is so rewarding and it will bring you joy to see the happiness you have brought to someone else's life.

Reiki dramatically improves your interactions and relationships with other people and helps you to see them as they really are, rather than being blinded by the image they put across or their false charm. Students often find after learning Reiki that they quickly re-evaluate their friendships with people, strengthening their relationships with those that value their friendship and drifting away from those that are merely draining their energy and taking advantage of them.

It is so easy to get trapped in the cycle of old lifestyle patterns and behaviours, for instance: following the same faddy diets that never ever work; making new years resolutions you know you won't stick to; making unrealistic demands on yourself either in work or personal relationships; struggling with financial issues or relationship problems. If you don't do something to break this cycle it is all too easy to continue this vicious cycle for your whole life.

Reiki can change the way you handle what life throws at you, in a way that is much more realistic and healthy for you. This won't necessarily be a conscious thing but you may find, for instance, that something that normally stressed you out now seems meaningless, or that you now won't give the time of day to someone who used to always take advantage of your kind nature. The changes can be very subtle and gradual or instantaneous. You learn to love yourself unconditionally, feel more at ease in your own skin and also learn to love others, but in a way that allows them to learn their own lessons from life, even if those lessons are sometimes harsh.

Usui-sensei stated that Reiki was the "art of inviting happiness." This is very true. Most people have no concrete understanding of what it means to be unequivocally happy. All too often in modern society our happiness is associated with wealth, material possessions or a successful career. Happiness is truly not about this. Real happiness comes from a profound understanding of the Universe and knowing your place in the Universe.

If you choose to learn Reiki and you whole-heartedly incorporate self-healing and responsible living into your every day life, you will be set on the path to enlightenment. For some this is a short and simple path, for others a much longer and rockier journey, but once you know you are on this path you will eventually find what true happiness is. Reiki is so much more than just a complementary therapy; it is The Way of The Universe.

Chapter Five

Why So Many Get It Wrong

There is a wealth of information about Usui Reiki Ryoho available in books and on the internet, yet much of it is based on either incorrect or misinterpreted information. Some information proclaiming to be 'traditional' Usui Reiki Ryoho obtained from living students of Usui-sensei, is traditional in the sense that Usui-sensei taught the student. However, some of the teachings pre-date his Reiki Ryoho, while the others are from different times in the development of Usui Reiki Ryoho.

A student of Usui-sensei's from the very start of his Reiki Ryoho teachings will possess a different understanding, with perhaps different techniques to a student at the end of Usui-sensei's development of Reiki Ryoho. There are many 'myths' and 'beliefs' that have come from a lack of in-depth understanding that are continually perpetuated and accepted as truth. Some of the main ones that diminish the effectiveness and therefore the professional standing of Reiki are:

"Reiki does not heal anything....it only allows the body to heal itself..."

"Reiki does not heal anything...it is purely a means of relaxation..."

"The energy is intelligent and goes where it needs to...."

"The practitioner is only a channel for the energy.....the less input in the treatment the practitioner has the better..."

"It does not matter what the practitioner thinks about during the treatment...."

"It does not matter what you do, it is your intention that counts..."

"Reiki works for the highest good and can do no harm..."

The biggest myth is that Reiki is a passive form of healing that does not treat or heal any conditions, medical or otherwise. Reiki simply works for the highest good and gives the client what they need (whatever that means). This is one of the biggest stumbling blocks in promoting Reiki within a medical environment. There is no truth to this. It only appears to be a fact because this is how many Reiki practitioners in the West use it.

Anyone that has studied Reiki and read any of Usui-sensei's words would know that this is not true. Here are some examples taken from Usui-sensei.

"...So if healer stares or breathes on or strokes with hands at the affected area such as toothache, colic pain, stomachache, neuralgia, bruises, cuts, burns and other swellings with pain will be gone. However a chronic disease is not easy, it's needed some time. But a patient will feel improvement at the first treatment..."[5]
"Any illness such as psychological or an organic disease can be cured by this method."[5]

"Usui Reiki Ryoho does not only heal illness. Mental illness such as agony, weakness, timidity, irresolution, nervousness and other bad habit can be corrected."[5]

"If brain disease occurs, I treat a head. If it's a stomachache, I treat a stomach. If it's an eye disease, I treat eyes."[5]

Even without any knowledge of Usui-sensei's words, any

competent Reiki practitioner should know from their own healing experiences that Reiki does indeed, treat and cause healing to take place for the many illnesses and injuries they have treated. Many Reiki teachers and practitioners unfortunately seem to ignore the words of Usui-sensei himself. As to why so many people get it wrong, we cannot give you an answer. All we can think of is that perhaps people are keen to avoid taking responsibility. By saying you are unable to treat a condition you are eliminating some self-responsibility and by doing this, any outcome becomes acceptable.

There are a number of reasons why Reiki as generally practiced today is now so far removed from the discipline developed by Usui-sensei:

❑ The Usui Reiki Ryoho Gakkai has kept a great deal of information within the confines of their association. This is not an excuse for poor practice among Western Reiki teachers though. There is enough good information available in the public domain for any competent Reiki teacher to be able to put together and teach an in-depth syllabus that covers the main teaching and methods of Usui Reiki Ryoho. The same is true for Reiki practitioners who want to work with Reiki in a professional and effective way.

❑ There is no set syllabus or course content for the different levels of Reiki, and there are no recognised formal qualifications for Reiki. This means Reiki teachers can teach whatever they want to on a Reiki course. Unfortunately this has created a situation where Reiki courses can vary greatly in quality, ranging from professional and well-developed courses to ones bordering on useless.

❑ The fact that Reiki can be taught in a few days and is such a simple system to learn and use has made it appear less awe-inspiring than it truly is. Today some people learn Reiki on a whim, with no thought of the amazing gift they are receiving. The discipline and commitment expected of students by Usui-sensei has all but disappeared. To use Reiki effectively takes time, effort and practice. Many hours of self-healing are required, ideally on a daily basis to develop and really understand Reiki.

❏ The belief that Reiki can be practiced and taught in any way, without any thought or reference to the original teachings and methods has allowed both Reiki teachers and practitioners to take Reiki away from its founding principles as a *healing and self-development system* and into the realms of a 'relaxation therapy' that anyone can practice without sufficient training, commitment or responsibility.

Having said that, there are many dedicated Reiki teachers and practitioners that are working with honesty and integrity to the best of their ability within the bounds of their training. With some time spent researching and locating more authentic information about the methods of Reiki practice, whether from books, the internet or other Reiki teachers, their work with Reiki can be greatly enhanced, both for themselves and their clients. With a desire to understand and enough time and effort, any Reiki teacher and practitioner can develop their knowledge and ability to a far higher standard and be closer to the original form of Reiki.

Chapter Six

How Reiki Works

As we have said, Reiki is a path to enlightenment, and as such, is the beginning of a wonderful spiritual journey of growth and development that leads ultimately to enlightenment and true happiness. Reiki is also a healing system, used originally to treat illnesses and injuries directly. Although this aspect of Reiki has changed over the years, we like to use Reiki as it was intended, and work to treat conditions in a direct or active way.

How Reiki functions is something that is becoming clearer as more research is carried out into different forms of energy healing. The mantra of many Reiki devotees is, "Reiki allows the body to heal itself." This is the explanation you will find in most Reiki books, and is the answer you will get from the majority of Reiki healers. What exactly does this mean? The stock answer, again favoured by most Reiki healers is that the energy brings the body into a form of energetic balance, which creates the appropriate conditions for the body to heal itself. Direct action on an illness or injury goes unmentioned. Yet, this is the primary method with which the Reiki energy works.

Fundamentally, Reiki Ryoho as used by Usui-sensei and his students worked by treating the illness or injury directly with energy to stimulate repair and recovery. Healing to achieve emotional and physical balance was a separate treatment that would be used once the illness or injury had been treated. This is the most effective way to work with the Reiki healing system.

We have seen the effectiveness of Reiki when used in this way over the many years of practicing Reiki. We have given healing treatments to people with a variety of illnesses and injuries, both physical and emotional with often amazing results. The actual mechanics of how Reiki works is something we are interested in. Some of the research and studies into energy and energy healing we have looked at are not only informative, but go a long way in explaining the mechanisms of how energy healing works. We describe Active Reiki as a way of working with energy in a focused way to directly treat any illness or injury, in the way of the founder of Reiki, Usui-sensei. There are a number of theories based on research that explain the different processes by which it is believed the direct effects of energy healing take place.

There are three main areas of research. The first is the field of Bioelectromagnetics, which studies the effects of man-made electromagnetic fields on biological processes. The second area is Bioelectromagnetism, which studies the electromagnetic effects of biological systems and the third is the study of natural energy healing methods. These are three distinctly different fields, but there is much that is common between them, there are even areas where there is convergence of theories and results. While it is beyond the scope of this book to go into any great depth into the science of energy healing, we would like to give an overview of some of the more relevant research.

The first thing we need to address is electromagnetic fields (EMF or EM fields) and explain what they are. EM fields are distinct physical fields produced by electrically charged objects. EM fields can be produced as a by-product of an electrical device, or they can be produced by electrical devices designed specifically for that purpose. For example, mobile phones, computers, electrical cables all have EM fields as an unwanted by-product, whereas Pulsed Electromagnetic Field Therapy devices are designed to produce specific EM fields. Biological systems, like the human body produce EM fields. Our bodies naturally emit EM fields from the heart, the brain and other endogenous current sources throughout our body. Electrocardiogram (ECG) and Electroencephalogram (EEG) are measurements of the electrical activity of the heart and the brain, which therefore produce EM fields. There is no longer any doubt in this. EM fields are defined in terms of their source densities. An EM field exists when a system contains source distributions of both charge and current densities. Every living thing has these two sources, which means that every living thing, by definition, has its own endogenous EM field.[6]

Energy healers, whether they are using Reiki, Qigong, Therapeutic Touch or any other modality, all produce EM fields as part of their healing practice. These EM fields are generally more coherent and therefore stronger than the ones naturally produced by the human body.

There are a number of studies that have documented the EM fields produced by a variety of energy healers. The most well known are by Seto et al.[7] and Zimmerman[8] that demonstrated the EM field produced by healers, Choi et al.[9] that demonstrated biophoton emissions from the hands, and Schwartz et al.[10] and Chien et al.[11] that confirmed the infra-red energy or heat produced by healers. This correlates with the experiences of Reiki practitioners that can feel heat, tingling or pulsing in their hands when they are working with the energy.

So, we know that electrical devices can be made to produce EM fields of variable frequency and power, and we know that Reiki practitioners when giving treatments produce EM fields, and when working in the traditional or Active way can produce EM fields of precise frequency and amplitude within the available range of frequencies.

The study of EM fields for use as a therapeutic tool began in Japan in the 1940's. There has also been extensive research in the former Soviet Union, Eastern European countries, and in the USA. There have been many studies into the healing effects of a variety of EM fields such as pulsed electromagnetic fields, static magnetic fields and high frequency EM fields, the results of which show that EM fields when applied at specific frequencies and amplitudes at the site of injuries stimulate repair and regeneration of a wide variety of both soft and hard tissue.[12,13,14]

Various EM field devices have been developed and introduced for medical use. In the USA, the Food and Drugs Administration (FDA) has approved specific frequencies of EM fields to be used to treat non-union and delayed fractures. There appears to be a creeping acceptance of EM field therapy as a healing tool among conventional medical practitioners. What is accepted now, is that weak EM fields can affect cells and stimulate repair of physical trauma, and there have been many studies undertaken which demonstrate this (see End Notes - Further Resources). The findings point to frequencies in the extremely low frequency range (ELF <300Hz) for physical healing of the body.[15,16] This fits nicely with Reiki, where we use the lower frequencies of the CKR (see Chapter 13) to work on injuries and illnesses of the physical body.

There have been a number of theories put forward to explain the mechanisms by which EM fields, both static (SMF) and pulsed (PEMF) interact with biological systems. Although these theories are based on EM fields produced by electrical and magnetic devices, there is no reason why the same principles will not apply to EM fields produced by Reiki practitioners. All of these theories have one thing in common; the EM field has a direct effect on the physically injured area, working at the cell level to instigate the repair process from within the damaged cells. How this happens has been studied and a number of interesting theories have been postulated.

Signal Transduction Pathways

Firstly, there is the study of the effects of EM fields on cell signal transduction pathways. Signal transduction refers to the process by which a living cell converts one type of signal into another, usually a biochemical reaction or series of reactions. In the case of EM field therapies, the instigating signal is electrical and/or magnetic and the response can be a biochemical cascade. This is a fascinating area of research that provides a mechanism to describe the healing effects of EM field therapies when applied to biological systems. For more detailed information it is worth reading the works of Dr Ross Adey, who has probably made the greatest contribution to this field of research (see End Notes - Further Resources). Dr Markov of Research International describes the process of EM field interaction at cellular level thus: "Looking on a cell, one may see the biological membrane as a first entity to interact with external electromagnetic fields. During these interactions alterations in the membrane electric charge distribution as well as in conformational status of the membrane constituents could occur. The alterations in the membrane properties are further transferred within cell interior via signal transduction pathways."

Some illnesses, such as cancer, diabetes and autoimmune problems can be caused by defects in the signal transduction pathways. It can be posited then that EM fields, which can work on the signal transduction pathways, can initiate or stimulate a healing reaction within the cells, which will affect and improve medical conditions.

The precise mechanism of how EM fields affect biological systems is still at the theoretical stage, but there are a number of important theories that give elegant solutions. There are models based on these theories that have been put forward to describe the possible mechanism of action of EM fields, and it is quite likely that more than one mechanism is involved, depending on the particular injury and pathology.

An excellent review of studies and theories of EM field therapies was written by Marko S. Markov.[17] In this paper Markov explains the different mechanisms of how weak EM fields affect biological processes. We have summarised some of the relevant points below:

One of the earliest models to describe the process by which exogenous EM fields could affect biological systems used an electromechanical model of the cell membrane. In this model it was assumed that non-thermal EM fields could affect ion binding and ion transport and affect the cascade of biological processes in individual cells that can cause tissue growth and repair.[18,19] How this actually happens in practice is still theoretical, but one possible mechanism is the rate of ion binding to receptor sites at the cell surface.[20]

Ion cyclotron resonance (ICR) was a theoretical development, which used AC (alternating current) and DC (direct current) magnetic fields to increase the mobility of specific ions.[21,22] This led to an ICR based device becoming commercially available for treating non-union fractures and spinal fusion.[23] The ICR model gained only limited acceptance because the thermal noise factor was not addressed. The problem was that energy associated with thermal noise is greater than the energy delivered by the applied EM field, i.e. the underlying EM fields created by the body are far stronger than the exogenous weak EM fields. It should not be possible for a weaker applied EM field to affect a charged ion moving under a stronger endogenous EM field. Basically, the applied EM field (below the thermal noise threshold) would be too weak to significantly affect the charge and cause a change in the ion binding or transport.[24]

The quantum mechanics based approach of Ion parametric resonance (IPR) was developed to resolve the thermal noise issue of ICR.[25] This was further developed over the next few years.[26,27,28]

The dynamical systems model sees the ion as having two energetically stable points, bound (in the molecular cleft at the inside edge of the cell) and unbound (in the Helmholtz plane). EM fields can affect the ratio of time spent bound to the time spent unbound.[20]

Whatever the mechanism by which weak EM fields affect ion binding and transport, the effects are well documented. There is strong experimentally observed evidence to support the significant biological effects of weak exogenous EM fields that act below the thermal noise threshold.[29,30,31,32,33,34,35,36,37,38]

Mobile Charge Interaction

Mobile charge interaction (MCI) is a theory based on the physical interactions between the magnetic field of the EM field and the moving charges within cells.[39] The magnetic field can change the velocity of the charge flow within a cell. If the charge flow is connected to, or part of, a biological function, then this change in velocity will cause a corresponding change in the biological function. For example, the charge flow can be associated with an enzyme, and therefore the magnetic field can change the enzyme reaction rates.[40,41] This mechanism has been posited for changes to biosynthetic events at the DNA level too, via electron velocity.[42,43,44]

Injury Currents

Another area of research involves currents of injury. At the site of injury to the musculoskeletal system an injury current is set up.[45] It has been found that this current plays a vital role in tissue repair and regeneration. As cells that are involved in the repair of traumatised tissue are electrically charged, endogenous EM fields can signal to these cells and cause them to migrate to the traumatised area.[46] It has been shown that negating the injury current effectively stops the repair process.[47] By extrapolation it can be postulated that by enhancing the current exogenously (through EM fields) the repair process should be accelerated. Dr. Markov speaking about EM fields and injury currents said "There is no better agent to interact with the injury current and restore normal functioning of the tissue than EMF." This has been demonstrated in effect by using electrical currents to force limb regeneration in rats.[48,49,50]

Biologically Closed Electric Circuits

Along similar lines to injury currents, it has been suggested that there are intrinsic electric pathways in the body. The Biologically Closed Electric Circuits (BCEC) hypothesis states that endogenous currents are set up when any pathological disorder occurs.[51] Furthermore, it should be possible to treat the disorders with exogenous electrical signals. This model was developed further to treat malignant tumours with electrotherapeutic techniques.[52,53]

Harmonic Frequency

An interesting concept is that of harmonic vibrations or frequencies. Fröhlich has posited that electric and elastic forces are interacting within the body at all times. This interaction will cause the molecules to vibrate at specific frequencies. These vibrations can become coherent, that is a number of molecules can vibrate or resonate at the same frequency and produce a far greater EM field than the sum of the individual molecules.[54,55]

There are two elements that need to be brought together to explain the EM field effect through harmonic frequency. Firstly, the body's cells can be seen as a tensegrity (tensional integrity) matrix. In fact, the entire body can be seen as a tensegrity matrix system.[56,57] A tensegrity structure is composed of discontinuous compression-resistant members that are not necessarily touching, connected by continuous tension cables.[58] What this means is the entire structure is made up of disconnected rigid members (such as girders or beams) that are held in place by tension cables rather than more rigid members. The integrity of the structure is dependent on the tension being continuous and the compression being discontinuous, i.e. the *continuous* pull of the cables is matched by the *discontinuous* pushing forces of the girders.

Secondly, following on from Fröhlich's work, Pienta and Coffey have found that cellular changes such as shape, motility and signal transduction occur within spatial and temporal harmonics that may be of regulatory importance, and that these vibrations can change when cells undergo changes, such as carcinogenesis. They posit that vibrational information can be transferred using the tissue tensegrity matrix made up of the nuclear matrix (the fibres around the inside of cells), the cytoskeleton (microfilaments that give shape to cells), and the extracellular matrix (structure that surrounds cells). This allows for information transfer in the form of chemome-chanical energy around the tissue tensegrity matrix and into the DNA itself. The mechanism they propose for this vibrational transfer is through the tensegrity matrix acting as a coupled harmonic oscillator (a system of masses connected by elastic elements in a three dimensional lattice) behaving as a signal trans-ducing system. For example, a physical trauma to one part of the body will transmit a vibrational signal throughout the tensegrity matrix around the body using harmonic wave motion.[59]

Signal transduction is a mechanism that can be used to initiate a healing response. As this occurs within a harmonic vibrational or frequency range, then it may be possible for an exogenous vibra-tional frequency signal applied at the appropriate vibrational frequency to initiate such a healing response.

One thing these theories have in common is the fact that precise frequencies of EM fields are required to give the desired healing results. With Active Reiki we aim to use the frequency needed to restore the damaged part of the body to its healthy state, so perhaps there is an element of all of these models in the process of healing with Reiki energy.

When Reiki practitioners say the energy is intelligent and it goes where it is needed, do they actually understand what this means? We have met many Reiki professionals through our work, and the agreed consensus among the vast majority is that the energy will travel around the body and go to the areas that are damaged and work effectively in those areas, regardless of where the practitioner puts their hands. They use this as a way of explaining why they do not need to know what is wrong with the client, because the energy will naturally go where it is needed. One of the other statements Reiki practitioners make is that Reiki does not actually heal any condition directly, rather it helps to relax the client which then allows the body to heal itself. This approach is very different from the way Usui-sensei practiced and taught Reiki, where, as we have stated already, the practitioner puts their hands (and therefore the energy) at the site of injury or illness to directly treat the problem.

We have called this method of working with Reiki energy, Passive Reiki, because the practitioner does not take an active role in the healing beyond channelling the energy into the client at either fixed or random hand positions with little or no regard to the energy needs of the client's illnesses or injuries. Working in this way will in fact help the client's body to heal itself. This particular method may not give recovery or regeneration at quite the same rate as working directly on the illnesses or injuries, but healing can be stimulated by this way of working.

Humoral Signalling

One such mechanism that could explain this type of healing is through humoral signalling. Theise and Bushell have proposed Melatonin as a possible mediator between the relaxation process and tissue repair and regeneration.[60] Although the study was based around relaxation through a variety of practices, such as Yoga and meditation, receiving Reiki treatments induces similar, if not deeper states of relaxation. What they have found is that stem cells or progenator cell components are found in virtually all the body's tissue and organs.

Furthermore, when a deep state of relaxation is induced, the levels of melatonin increase.[61] Melatonin has been found to have a number of beneficial effects. It has been found that melatonin plays a key role in the regeneration of specific areas of the body, such as the liver,[62] skin,[63,64] hair,[64,65] the brain,[66,67] the eyes and ocular system,[68] the heart,[69,70] the GI tract/endothelium,[71] the neuroendocrine-reproductive axis,[72] and the muscles.[73,74] Melatonin also possesses protective properties that help protect against oxidative and other types of stress.[75]

Beyond helping to fight stress and regenerate and repair both healthy and damaged tissue and organs, melatonin has also been found to induce apoptosis, (a form of self-destruction) in malignant cells such as in the breast, lungs, ovaries, prostate, stomach as well as others.[76,77,78]

Chapter Seven

Passive and Active Reiki Healing

Passive Reiki Healing

It is not universally agreed precisely how Reiki actually works but generally Reiki is regarded as being a passive form of healing by the majority of Reiki practitioners and teachers. What this means is they believe the energy will work without any input or direction from the practitioner.

The claim made by many Reiki practitioners worldwide is that the energy used in Reiki is intelligent, will know what to treat, go where it is needed, and work for the highest good. So, practitioners using passive Reiki trust in the energy to work without their guidance or influence, and will put as little input into the healing as possible, acting purely as channels for the energy. Some may use a form of 'scanning' or be intuitively guided to work on certain parts of the body, but even so, they will not consciously adjust the frequency of the energy, preferring to allow the energy flow in a more general way. Their theory is that the less *they* do themselves the better, because by having any input into the healing they would adversely affect the path of the energy. There is the common belief that it is better not to concentrate or be focused when giving Reiki treatments, even when treating serious illnesses or injuries. This form of Reiki practice believes that by being focused the practitioner is stifling the energy flow, and it is better for the practitioner to think of something else while healing.

Some Reiki practitioners believe that it is better not to work on treating any illness or injury because they would not know what would be in the client's highest good. They believe only God, or the client's higher self, could possibly know what would need to be treated. For many practitioners Reiki is not even considered a therapy or a healing system or even a treatment but a way of allowing the body to heal itself, or not, depending on every individual's path and higher good.

The practitioner will often place their hands in a set series of positions around the body remaining in each position for a similar length of time, regardless of where the injury or illness is located. They allow the energy to define its own course within the body, saying that the body will take as much energy as it requires, where it requires it.

Some practitioners arbitrarily insist that certain parts of the body will always need more healing time than the other parts. For instance, we have heard of a teacher who always insists that the back of the head needs fifteen minutes healing, where as the other parts of the body only need three minutes each. There are other practitioners that only ever treat the head and ignore the rest of the body completely.

Specific conditions are not generally addressed using passive healing, and when they are, the appropriate frequency of energy is not used in a deliberate way. Illnesses, injuries or any other factors are not taken into consideration and it is claimed that the healing will always be for the highest good, as there are never any contraindications with Reiki. Even when specific conditions are being treated, the energy is channelled in a passive way with no effort to use the optimum frequency.

The overriding factor with passive Reiki is the belief that it is the practitioner's intention to 'work for the highest good' that is important, their actual actions and thoughts are irrelevant and will make no difference to the healing. It is this one principle alone that makes passive Reiki as far removed from Usui Reiki Ryoho as is possible.

Active Reiki Healing

The reason we have coined the phrase 'Active Reiki Healing' is to differentiate between the modern concept of Western (passive) Reiki practice and the traditional method of (active) Reiki healing. Reiki was developed and used by Usui-sensei as an effective healing method to treat any illness or injury directly. When or why this has been lost from traditional Reiki is something we cannot answer.

The only way to use Reiki effectively is to treat the presenting illness or injury directly. Of course, where there is emotional trauma, which may be causing or aggravating the illness or injury, it is necessary to treat the emotional trauma as well. To have a direct effect on the illness, injury or the emotional trauma it is vital to use the correct frequency that will support the repair and regeneration process. This is achieved by using the relevant shirushi (symbol) with its jumon/kotodama (name/mantra). So for physical conditions use the CKR and for mental/emotional use the SHK. If the shirushi are used in white, they give the frequency range for either the physical (CKR) or the mental/emotional (SHK) body. You can be even more precise with the frequency by using the shirushi in specific colours to give a more exact frequency. Determining the correct colour for the shirushi can be an intuitive or guided choice, or it can be a practical and mechanical process. Once you have determined the most effective frequency you can add focused intention and visualisation to the treatment. By using focused intent you can direct the energy to work on improving the condition you are treating. This will help to improve the outcome of the treatment by further enhancing the repair and regeneration process.

This is by far the most effective way to use Reiki. By working in this manner you are focusing all your efforts on helping the person you are treating, as much as you possibly can, within the limits of the Universe.

Why Use Active Reiki

First of all, taking an active role in healing is not playing God, as many Reiki practitioners claim, it is simply giving your clients the best possible treatment you can within the limits of the Universe. If you treat someone actively and then the client still does not respond, you have at least done everything you possibly could to help that person. Doctors take an active role in treating people on a daily basis all over the world and we do not accuse them of playing God, so why should a Reiki practitioner who works actively be playing God?

Usui-sensei, the founder of Reiki, treated conditions directly and he did not use a set series of hand positions. He said himself in the Usui Reiki Hikkei (Usui Reiki Handbook) that, "If brain disease occurs I treat the head. If it's a stomach ache I treat the stomach. If it's an eye disease I treat the eyes."[5] We follow his example. If someone has a tumour in their liver and you treat their head, there could be numerous blockages between their head and liver, which take the energy away from the condition that needs treating. In addition to that, the frequency of energy needed to treat the head could be very different to the frequency needed to treat the tumour. For these reasons it is much more effective to treat the condition directly.

If an individual comes to a practitioner with a specific condition, the practitioner should deal with that condition directly. It is selling Reiki short to say that the energy simply helps the body to heal itself. Reiki heals directly, Usui-sensei said so himself, and we know this to be the case from all the work we have done.

Passive Reiki healing means that the practitioner can take as little responsibility for the welfare of the client as possible and is very probably why some people deem Reiki as a 'flaky' therapy. Many other more accepted therapies have more stringent standards and Reiki should have too if it is to be properly accepted by the medical community and the public at large.

What Active Reiki actually means in practice is that you are treating conditions directly by channelling energy at the frequency needed by the condition being treated. If a client presents an Active Reiki healer with a damaged bone, the healer will work on that bone. We in addition use intention and visualisation, which has been proven to maximise the benefits of the healing process.

With passive Reiki healing, the entire healing energy spectrum is being channelled into the client containing all frequencies of energy. This means that a small percentage of those frequencies are working on the actual condition, whilst the rest of the energy is being wasted because it is not directly treating the condition being dealt with. By healing actively, energy is being channelled at a specific frequency, meaning that all the energy channelled is used to work on a specific condition and none of the energy is being wasted. This is achieved by using the Reiki shirushi (symbols), which filter the energy, narrowing down the frequency range and then colour is added to the shirushi to narrow down the frequency range even further.

We acknowledge that the physical, emotional and spiritual bodies are interconnected and interdependent so a physical condition for example may be caused or aggravated by an emotional trauma, but you need different energies to treat the physical symptom and the emotional cause. It is much more effective to concentrate all the energy on healing the primary presenting symptom first and then deal with the underlying causes afterwards. This is, of course, assuming there is physical damage to heal first. Where a presenting pain is not linked to physical damage or injury and is purely caused by emotional trauma, we will treat the emotional trauma directly, which tends to stop the pain.

Chapter Eight

Visualisation and Intention

When working with the Reiki energy for healing purposes, the main factor that determines the effectiveness of the treatment is the frequency of the energy being channelled relative to the frequency needed by the condition. By using the required frequency, the energy can work directly on the condition. Two other factors can also provide added benefit to the healing process, intention and visualisation.

While an Active Reiki healer is using Reiki on either themselves, or a client, they will always use intention and visualisation in addition to the Reiki energy. Intention and visualisation can speed up the healing process dramatically. A good Reiki practitioner should be focused during their healing, concentrating intently on the healing process and visualising the condition getting better, as well as constantly fixing or affirming their intention.

There are many studies in the field of Psychoneuroimmunology (the relationship between the mind, brain and immune system) that prove the link between the mind and the body. It is generally and widely accepted now that the mind can produce profound physiological changes within the body. There have been many studies that have looked at emotional factors and illnesses. The originator of this field of study is experimental psychologist Robert Ader, Ph.D. His most famous experiment, 'Behaviourally conditioned immunosuppression' used a distinctive taste administered with an immunosuppressive drug given to rats.[79] The immunosuppressive drug caused nausea in the rats. The drug was then stopped, but the taste was still administered. The rats continued to get sick and some died, demonstrating that the taste alone was enough to suppress the rats' immune systems. This effectively proved the power the mind has over the immune system and paved the way for more interest and research in this area.

There have also been studies that have looked at focused intention and visualisation on biological systems outside of the body. A number of studies around the title: 'Effect of Conscious Intention on Human DNA' were undertaken by Dr Glen Rein PH.D to look at the effect of focused and non-focused intention on biological systems.[80] All the tests were carried out on in-vitro tumour cell cultures and isolated human DNA in test tubes. Both energy healers and non-healers were used in these studies. We have summarised some of the findings of this study below:

The first study was designed to look at the effects of a range of both focused and non-focused intentions and visualisations on in-vitro tumour cells. For this experiment a healer, Leonard Laskow and a non-healer as a control, worked on sets of three petri dishes containing the same number of tumour cells. The experiment called on the 'healers' to use five distinct intentions and two visualisations. Each of the intentions and visualisations was used both individually and in combination.

The intentions used were:

1. *"Returning to the natural order and harmony of the cell's normal rate of growth"* i.e. before they were transformed to tumor cells.

2. *"Circulating the microcosmic orbit"*

3. *"Letting God's will flow through his hands"* i.e. a transpersonal intention.

4. *"Unconditional love"* i.e. no specific direction to the energy was

given.

5. *"Dematerialization into the light and/or dematerialization into the void"'*

The two visualisations used were:

1. Only three tumour cells left in the petri dish

2. Many more tumour cells in the petri dish.

The results of the experiments showed that using unconditional love had no effect at all, but the most effective focused intention combined with an effective visualisation gave a tumour cell growth inhibition of 40%. The focused intention Laskow found to be the most effective was *"returning to the natural order and harmony of the cell's normal rate of growth"*. The visualisation used was a mental image of only a few cells in the petri dish.

Using the intention *"returning to the natural order and harmony of the cell's normal rate of growth"* without the visualisation gave an inhibition of cell growth of 20%.

When Laskow used visualisation without focused intention, the image of only three tumour cells remaining gave an inhibition of cell growth of 18%. Conversely, the visualisation of many more tumour cells gave an increase of cell growth of 15%.

The other important study used Leonard Laskow to test the effect of directed intention, unconditional love and specific visualisations on human DNA in test tubes. Laskow was able to cause both winding and unwinding of DNA by simply changing his directed intention and visualisation.

In another study Modulation of DNA conformation by heart-focused intention[81] carried out at the Institute of HeartMath (IHM), non-healers used specific HeartMath techniques to promote positive and loving feelings around the heart area, which create a state of calmness that leads to a more coherent heart rhythm. The heart itself creates an EM field and this field is affected by the heart's rhythm. It has been postulated that the EM field from the heart can energetically mediate well-being and healing. A group of non HeartMath practitioners were used as a control. We have summarised the relevant details of the study below:

The participants were monitored for their heart rate variable to assess the heart coherence of each individual. Each participant held the test tube containing the human DNA sample for a similar and specified time frame. They used the intention to wind or unwind the DNA as directed.

The HeartMath trained group worked in three states:

1. Using focused intention to alter the DNA while generating feelings of love and appreciation i.e. in heart focused state to create high levels of coherence.

2. Having no focused intention to alter the DNA while generating feelings of love and appreciation i.e. in heart focused state to create high levels of coherence.

3. Using focused intention to alter the DNA but in their normal state i.e. with low levels of coherence.

The control group used focused intention to alter the DNA while generating feelings of love and appreciation i.e. in heart focused state.

The HeartMath trained group tested in the first state using focused intention (see above) achieved greater heart coherence and demonstrated between 10-25% in changes in DNA conformation. The control group did not show a significant increase in heart coherence and achieved no significant (1%) change in DNA conformation.

When the HeartMath trained participants were tested in the second state using no focused intention (see above) they showed the same level of DNA conformation as the control group.

When the HeartMath trained participants were tested in the third state using focused intention without increased heart coherence (see above) they showed no significant level of change in DNA conformation.

This quite clearly shows both the effectiveness and importance of focused and directed intention and visualisation when giving Reiki treatments. It is vitally important to direct the energy using focused intention and visualisation when giving Reiki treatments, to maximise the healing potential of the energy and give the greatest improvement to the condition being treated.

Even people that are not trained healers can learn to use focused intention and visualisation by firstly attaining a deeply relaxed state and then applying the same principles.

These studies demonstrate that the most effective method for healing is to combine focused intention and visualisation with the directed Reiki energy. Healing in this focused way the results are very often phenomenal. This way of working is more in line with the original teachings and methods of Usui-sensei.

Chapter Nine

Facts and Myths About Reiki

Due to the tradition of secrecy within Japanese culture, the lack of available historical written documentation and the lack of living students of Usui-sensei, we have in reality very little information about how Usui-sensei worked. There seems to have been a lot of Chinese whispers going on over the years about how Reiki actually operates.

A lot of well meaning people have misinterpreted the information given to us by original students of Usui-sensei, some of whom studied his older teachings before his satori and discovery of Reiki. To further compound the situation, some people have 'made up' their own style of Reiki with new symbols and some have trademarked their own styles of Reiki. A whole barrage of myths has been developed about this healing system that we are keen to dismiss. Below you can find the facts and myths about Reiki to help you separate the wheat from the chaff when you go on your Reiki journey.

Myth

It is a widely held myth that Reiki was re-discovered by Usui-sensei and that Reiki is an ancient form of healing.

Fact

Usui-sensei discovered Reiki whilst on retreat on Mount Kurama in Japan. This is believed to have taken place in 1922, although other dates have been suggested. On the twenty-first day of his retreat, after much time spent praying, meditating and fasting, Usui-sensei was given the Reiki cure by God (or the Universe, the terminology is really not important). He was also given, or developed, the Reiki symbols to use for channelling energy. Usui-sensei said himself that "My Reiki Ryoho is an original method...I've never been given this method by anybody..."

The mistake people commonly make, is placing every kind of healing under the same umbrella. Healing has been around as long as people have. There have always been people with a natural healing gift, then, as now, there are people that have 'healing hands', people that can naturally channel energy for healing purposes. Usui Reiki Ryoho on the other hand, has been around since Usui-sensei discovered it. There were of course many different forms of energy healing prior to Reiki and there continue to be many different forms of energy healing today, some of these are called Reiki despite having nothing to do with Usui-sensei what so ever.

Reiki, as discovered, developed and practiced by Usui-sensei is unique and exclusively his system. Reiki as a healing therapy is a complete system of healing, allowing healing on all levels, physical, emotional and spiritual. Any one can be attuned or connected to the source of the energy and can be given the gift of healing in a short space of time with the teachings of Usui-sensei.

Myth

There are many myths regarding the origins of Reiki. Many people say that Reiki originated in Tibet, China, Egypt or India and some people claim that the symbols used in Reiki have been found in Tibetan monasteries or temples in other countries.

Fact

Reiki is a Japanese healing system and the Reiki symbols are of Japanese origin. There are forms of energy healing that do originate in China, such as Qi Gong healing, but that bears no relation to Reiki, and any healing systems that were practiced in ancient Egypt or India were not Reiki as we know it. There is no use of Reiki in Tibetan medicine nor is there anything similar to Reiki used in Tibetan medicine. Reiki does not have any ties with Tibetan culture or medicine. Just because some symbols were drawn in a temple that look similar to the Reiki symbols, it does not mean that there is any connection between the two. Tibetan Reiki was developed in America and has no foundations in Tibet whatsoever. Reiki is a unique discovery by Usui-sensei.

Myth

There are widespread claims amongst Reiki teachers and practitioners that the symbols used in Reiki are merely a focus for intent, or that they are only for students that are unable to connect to the energy through intent. The symbols are seen to be part of a ritual that teaches the student to invoke a certain kind of energy, but the symbols themselves have no power or purpose. They are either viewed in effect as training wheels that can be discarded by students once they become more proficient at their healing work.

Frequently, the physical energy symbol (CKR), the emotional energy symbol (SHK) and the oneness symbol (HSZSN) are used in a kind of symbol or Reiki 'sandwich' to treat the client, combining all the energies in one fail swoop. Yet other Reiki teachers do not believe that the symbols are needed at all because all that matters is intention.

Fact

However the symbols were discovered, developed or given to Usui-sensei, they are an integral part of the practice and teaching of Reiki. The symbols are used to connect to specific and precise vibrations or frequencies of energy. Working without the symbols and their jumon and kotodama makes it incredibly difficult to effectively treat any illness or injury. For most Reiki practitioners that work in a passive way, it is difficult, and for some impossible to channel energy into their clients other than in a way similar to spiritual healing, with no regards for the conditions that require treatment. You cannot honestly deem yourself to be a Reiki practitioner if you are in effect working as a spiritual healer. The symbols and their jumon and kotodama essentially define Reiki.

Usui did not start teaching the use of the symbols he was given until 1923. One reason for this is that his teachings changed over a period of time from his earlier healing methods to his Reiki Ryoho. The change was gradual as his new method developed and evolved through his practice.

The symbols CKR and SHK narrow down the frequency range of the energy you are using, allowing you to channel energy at the correct frequency for every condition you could ever need to treat. The way the symbol is drawn and the colour of the symbol defines the frequency of the energy you will be using to heal with. The symbols must be drawn correctly because their geometry dictates the frequency of the energy you will be channelling. If you draw them incorrectly, you will use the incorrect frequency.

It has been shown that the various parts of the body will respond to precise electromagnetic frequencies and will repair when these frequencies are applied.[12] Therefore it makes perfect sense that when we heal we should use the correct frequency to initiate repair in the condition we are treating.

A student of Hayashi explained this very same thing in an article written in 1928, "I have experienced/researched some treatments but Reiki is the best as far as I know. Reiki is the most unique and the most effective, it can really heal any disease.........when my hands with activated blood are put on the patient's body, I think my blood vibration may promote the patient's blood vibration. Blood current, vibration may become the same" ("A Treatment to Heal Diseases, Hand Healing" by Shouoh Matsui in the magazine 'Sunday Mainichi', Mar. 4, 1928).

There are very few, if any, people that do not need to use the symbols for healing. You would need to be able to intuitively vary the frequency of the energy you are using and there are not many individuals enlightened enough to do that.

An extra point worth making is that the CKR and SHK symbols should not be used together to heal as the frequencies may clash, which may cause your clients to feel nauseas or ill.

Myth

Some say that the Reiki symbols can be shown to anyone and plastered anywhere and it does not matter who sees them because no harm can come of this.

Fact

In keeping with Japanese tradition, as Reiki teachers we should respect the founder of Reiki and his teachings. In Japan, the methods of Reiki are still only shared with Reiki students. We should have the same approach to Reiki in the West.

As previously discussed, the Reiki symbols and their respective jumon/kotodama (name/mantra) invoke a certain kind of energy. To use this energy in keeping with Usui-sensei's teachings requires training in the techniques and methods of Reiki. The Reiki symbols, like all the teachings of Reiki, should be treated with respect and only shown to those at the appropriate level in their Reiki path. If some untrained individual sees a Reiki symbol on some website and thinks, "oh that looks easy I will have a go at that by myself," they may potentially cause themselves or others harm through a lack of understanding.

Playing with energy when you do not know what you are doing can be damaging or harmful. We have heard about a Reiki teacher who used to virtually knock people over with Reiki energy as a kind of 'trick' and demonstration of his power over them. Just because you may use energy for good and responsibly it does not mean that everyone else will do the same. Out of respect for Usui-sensei and to protect yourself and others, only show the Reiki symbols to qualified Reiki practitioners and teachers.

Myth

There is no 'right' way or 'wrong' way to practice Reiki, it is up to each individual practitioner how they work. What matters is the practitioner's intention.

Fact

This is something that is believed by many Reiki practitioners and teachers we have come across. Their belief is that Reiki can be practiced any way they want to as long as they have good intentions. This belief is an extension of 'the energy is intelligent and always works for the highest good' myth. To us it demonstrates a lack of understanding of the system of Reiki.

The system of Reiki is based on specific techniques and methods that are underpinned by a required level of knowledge, understanding and practical ability. Teaching or practicing Reiki without this fundamental core of knowledge and techniques renders the practice ineffective and a poor imitation of Reiki. It is akin to an individual swinging their leg forward or throwing a punch and believing they are practising Karate. Each system of Karate teaches specific and precise techniques that define the system, simply throwing an arm or leg forward is not Karate. Similarly, putting your hands on or above someone does not make it Reiki, what makes it Reiki are the attunements, the teachings and the practice of the Reiki methods.

Myth

It is yet another widely held myth that Reiki does not heal directly but is purely a tool for allowing the body to restore itself to optimum health. The healer's hands, so it is said, can be placed anywhere on the body and the 'intelligent' energy will heal the person where and how it is most needed. The healer does not try to treat any condition. The less input the healer has into the healing the better, as they are merely channels for the energy. Allegedly they don't need to concentrate and their mind can drift anywhere, at any time during the healing, as the healing basically takes care of itself. Other healers say that a set series of standard hand positions are required for any and every client.

Fact

Using Reiki in this way is not making effective use of this extraordinary healing system. As you have read earlier in the book, working actively with the energy, concentrating and using visualisation and intention will maximise the healing process. The potential of Reiki is limitless, but all too often we come across the colossal constraints people place on this amazing energy healing system. By stipulating that the energy is 'intelligent' and the practitioner should have no input, all the responsibility is transferred away from the practitioner and put onto the Reiki energy.

Effectively in these circumstances the practitioner can do as they please, without liability, because they are not making any real commitment to help their clients. What is the point of going to a service provider who does not really offer you a service? Clients go for a Reiki treatment to feel better, to see results, to change their lives. It is the Reiki practitioner's responsibility to treat their client's most urgent conditions and within their remit, help them get healthy and back on their own two feet as empowered individuals. We were all given intelligence and the ability to heal for a reason and it makes sense logically and intuitively to do everything within our power as Reiki practitioners to help our clients when they come to us for healing. By healing in an active way, you can be sure that you are doing this.

Myth

You will no doubt hear it said by many Reiki practitioners that Reiki can do no harm; it has no contraindications, and always works for the highest good. Some healers will say that if they make any mistakes during the healing their spirit guides or the Universe will correct these for them.

Fact

Reiki has contraindications in much the same way as other complementary therapies do. As a Reiki practitioner you have a responsibility to establish what medical conditions your client is suffering from, what medications they are taking and the implications a Reiki treatment will have on these factors. As an example, if you are treating a diabetic person who takes insulin for their condition and you improve the function of their pancreas, stimulating the bodies own insulin production, the person will require a lower level of insulin when they inject themselves.

Therefore it is vital to inform the client that they must check their insulin levels after the treatment and before they take their insulin injections. This sort of reasoning applies for other sorts of conditions and in some cases it is necessary to work with the individual's doctor on monitoring the results of the healing process so the doctor can adjust the dosage of their medication accordingly. We cannot emphasise enough that it is your responsibility as a practitioner to be aware of everything when treating your clients, such as doctor's instructions, medication and the law regarding Reiki. A Reiki practitioner is not just an inert channel but an active participant in the healing process. Of course you will always work for the highest good and a major part of this means being practical and accepting the reality of the situation you are presented with. TAKE RESPONSIBILITY.

Myth

There are a number of Reiki practitioners and teachers that specify a fixed time gap between taking level 1 and level 2 courses. They say that a certain amount of time is necessary to become au fait with the energy and to practice healing and the skills already given.

Fact

This myth would make sense were if it were not for the poor comprehension of Reiki many people have. It makes sense that students will need time to practice and develop the skills they have been given, but this ideally should be with the complete teachings of level 1 and level 2 rather than with half the teachings given at level 1. Reiki level 1 teaches you only how to use 'Rei' energy to heal yourself, spiritually. It does not teach the use of the shirushi (symbols) to allow you to heal any physical or emotional problems. Therefore, many people learn level 1 and become frustrated when they can only heal to a certain degree.

We recommend that most students learn level 1 and 2 together so that they have the tools to heal themselves straight away, on a physical, emotional and spiritual level. This way, they can more rapidly heal themselves through their cleansing process and have the ability to directly heal their own as well as others conditions.

Hiroshi Doi has stated that Hayashi taught the level 1 and 2 courses together. The time delay is futile at best and at worst counter productive to the student's self development and healing progress. A student of Reiki can very quickly become disillusioned if they are misled to believe that they can walk away after their level 1 course and heal anything. By learning the courses together the student leaves with a practitioner qualification and the ability to heal themselves and others in the best way possible. The time for us all to be fulfilling our higher purpose on Earth is now and senseless time constraints on taking a Reiki 2 course will only delay people's self development.

Chapter Ten

The Levels of Reiki

The Original Reiki Ryoho System

In Usui-sensei's original teachings there were many more levels to his Reiki Ryoho teachings than the three or four that are generally taught today. This is something most Reiki researchers and historians agree on, however, where there is disagreement, is with the actual number of levels Usui-sensei taught in his Reiki Ryoho. There is evidence for four[2], five, six[2], seven, even thirteen[2] main levels with sub-levels within each main level. It is very likely the levels Usui-sensei taught would have changed as his teachings developed and changed. Reiki Ryoho developed as a system and changed from Usui-sensei's earlier teachings with his satori on Mt Kurama. His teachings after his satori are what we would recognise as Reiki Ryoho. What we do know is Usui-sensei was a martial-artist and he mixed with other martial arts experts, so it is very likely that he would have used a similar grading system for his Reiki Ryoho as he used for his martial arts. We feel the seven level system as described below is probably the closest to Usui-sensei's teaching system as used by the Usui Reiki Ryoho Gakkai, with level 6 and 7 specific to the Gakkai. We believe Usui-sensei's students that taught external to the Gakkai would have used a similar system, but without level 6 and 7, making it a five level system. The 7 main levels were as follows:

Level 1 - Shoden First Teachings

This starts a student's Reiki journey and gives the first part of the

Reiki energy. The emphasis is on self-healing and self-development. The way of healing at this level is through the use of the high frequency Rei energy, the 'light' component of Reiki. Specific techniques are taught at this level, which need to be practiced until proficient. There are four attunements given to the student for this level.

Level 2 - Okuden Second Teachings

This continues and builds from the first teachings to give the second part of the Reiki energy. The emphasis is still on self-healing and self-development, with the addition of healing others. The prime way of healing at this level is through the lower frequency energies accessed with the shirushi (symbols) and their jumon (name) and kotodama (mantra), the 'Ki' component of Reiki. Specific techniques are taught at this level, which need to be practiced until proficient. There is one attunement given for this level.

Level 3 - Shinpiden Mystery Or Hidden Teachings

This level contains teachings that go beyond the realms of energy healing, hence they are called the mysterious teachings.

This level is taught to students that have shown commitment and ability with their Reiki practice and demonstrated 'right thinking and right living'. This level contains teachings in mysticism, spirituality, psychic development and specialist healing methods. Students would specialise in one area, generally their area of ability or gift.

Level 4 - Shihan-Kaku Beginner Teacher

This is the level at which a student would be allowed to teach Reiki. At this level they would be able to teach up to level 4, but they could only teach the relevant level 3 subject of their specialisation. To achieve this level a student would have to have great knowledge and ability in at least one subject area from level 3 as well as the knowledge and ability from level 1, 2 and 4. Of course embracing 'right thinking and right living' is essential. The Master attunement is given at this level.

Level 5 - Shihan-Sensei Expert Reiki Teacher

This is a highly respected level within Reiki. To achieve this level a student would have to have great knowledge and ability in all the subject areas from level 3, as well as the knowledge and ability from level 1, 2 and 4. The title of Shihan-sensei is a term of great respect and has to be earned. This title is used by students for their teacher as a sign of their respect for their teacher. Of course embracing 'right thinking and right living' is essential.

Level 6 - By Invitation Only

Level 6 is an honorary grade awarded for service to Reiki. This level is open only to members of the Usui Reiki Ryoho Gakkai.

Level 7 - By Invitation Only

Level 7 is an honorary grade awarded for service to Reiki. This level is open only to members of the Usui Reiki Ryoho Gakkai.

The Modern Usui Reiki Ryoho Gakkai System

The modern form of Usui Reiki Ryoho practiced by the Usui Reiki Ryoho Gakkai today is believed to have six levels in total. There are three main levels, within which there are sub-levels or levels of proficiency, which have specific techniques that need to be practiced and mastered by the student before moving on to the next level.[2] It is believed these teachings are much closer to Usui-sensei's original Reiki, with the focus on self-development and spiritual growth as much as on healing.

Level 1 - Shoden First Teachings

This is similar to the Shoden taught by Usui-sensei. There may be some changes to the original system, but these would be minimal. We do not know the full syllabus for this level, as this information is kept within the Gakkai. We do know that the emphasis is on self-development as well as self-healing. Specific techniques are taught at this level within each sub-level, which need to be practiced until proficient.

Level 2 - Okuden Second Teachings

Again this level is similar to the okuden taught by Usui-sensei. There are sub-levels within the main level that need to be practiced and mastered. In line with Japanese culture, the teachings of Usui-sensei would be honoured and practiced now as they were in his day. Any variation would be kept to a minimum. The emphasis is still on self-development and healing. Additional techniques are introduced at this level, with a wider range of knowledge covering more areas.

Level 3 - Shinpiden Mystery Or Hidden Teachings

It is believed this level contains the higher levels of Usui-sensei's teachings that have been amalgamated into this level. These go beyond the realms of energy healing, hence they are called the mysterious teachings. This level contains teachings in many areas, including mysticism, spirituality, psychic development and specialist healing methods. There are sub-levels within this level with specific techniques and knowledge.

The Western Reiki System

Western Reiki has adopted the three level system for Reiki teaching introduced by Dr Hayashi and Mrs Takata. Many of the mystery teachings and some other methods and techniques were discarded by Dr Hayashi. The rest of the teachings were incorporated into the remaining three levels.

It is easy to see why Dr Hayashi did this, he was a medical man with perhaps little time for the more esoteric elements of Reiki Ryoho and both he and Usui-sensei wanted to simplify the teachings so virtually anyone would be able to learn the system. It is our belief that he made these changes with the knowledge and blessing of Usui-sensei to ensure his Reiki Ryoho teachings would progress beyond the spiritually evolved to the majority of ordinary people.

Level 1 Beginner

This is very similar to the Shoden level taught by Usui-sensei. There are some techniques that heave been removed and some that have been adapted. The knowledge taught at this level is generally not as in-depth as the original Shoden level. This is seen as the beginner level and teaches the student to self-heal with the Rei energy. There are four attunements at this level generally, although some systems have a different number.

Level 2 Practitioner

This is similar to the Okuden level taught by Usui-sensei. Again, some techniques have been taken out while others have been adapted. The symbols are taught at this level and the student learns how to treat others. There is one attunement with this course commonly, but there can be variations to this, depending on the system. This is regarded as the practitioner course, which allows students to practice Reiki professionally.

Level 3 Master/Teacher

This is called the master or master/teacher level. The student learns how to teach Reiki and attune others. The student usually receives one attunement on this course and learns about the master symbol, but some systems have more attunements and even more than one master symbol. This course is probably the one that is furthest from the original. Many techniques and a great deal of knowledge have been removed from Usui-sensei's original teachings.

Chapter Eleven

Japanese Versus Western Reiki

Japanese Reiki

The tem 'Japanese Reiki' is often used to describe the forms of Reiki that were taught and practiced in Japan originally and are based on Usui Reiki Ryoho with Usui-sensei as the originator. Japanese Reiki cannot be defined within a framework of one set of teachings or practices. There is not one single form that is 'Japanese Reiki'. Instead there are many forms of Reiki that originated with Usui-sensei.

The students that studied with Usui-sensei did so at different times during the development of his Reiki Ryoho, so there would have been differences in the methods and techniques they would have learned. As these students went on to become teachers in their own right, their teachings reflected these differences. As teachers, some of these students added their own interpretations and knowledge to the teachings in the shape of altered and new techniques. So we are left with a variety of 'Japanese Reiki' systems that owe their existence to Usui-sensei, and have evolved and developed over the years.

All of these systems of Reiki are equally valid and relevant, though how close they are to the teachings of Usui-sensei we cannot comment upon. The original teachings of Usui-sensei are, we believe, still available within the Usui Reiki Ryoho Gakkai. Hopefully one day these teachings will be made public to ensure Usui-sensei's legacy continues as he had wished.

Western Reiki

The term 'Western Reiki' is often used to refer to the forms of Reiki that are generally taught outside of Japan and are either from the Takata lineage, if they are based on Usui Reiki, or from an originator other than Usui-sensei if they are not. The blanket term 'Western Reiki' covers many hundreds of forms of Reiki, some recognisable as Reiki and some so far removed from Usui-sensei's system that it is a misnomer to call them Reiki.

The fragmentation of Reiki in the West started with the death of Mrs Takata. She had taught 22 masters/teachers and some of them formed the Reiki Alliance that sought to continue Mrs Takata's teachings as authentically as they could, even down to charging the same fees for their Reiki courses. The other masters/teachers went their own ways and adapted Mrs Takata's teachings with new techniques and knowledge that they developed themselves.

This tradition of masters/teachers changing the form of Reiki they were taught continues today, hence the large number of styles and forms of Reiki in existence. This is a more Western concept, as traditionally in Japan students would respect the teachings of their sensei to a much higher degree and try to stay true to the original system as much as they could.

Reiki practitioners and teachers generally say that Japanese Reiki is more intuitive and spiritual than Western Reiki. The system of Reiki that originally came to the West was from Dr Hayashi's lineage, which was a more practical and clinical method compared to the earlier more complex esoteric teachings of Usui-sensei. There were obvious cultural differences between Western society and Japanese society in the early 20th century, which account for some of the changes and omissions, and any other differences are due to the line of Western Reiki teachers.

With Western Reiki the focus is on healing with very simple and easy techniques that give results in a short time. With Japanese Reiki there is the same element of healing to achieve a cure in a short time, but there is also an element of self-development through specific techniques that allow the student to grow and develop, in a spiritual sense, as well as heal on a physical and emotional level.

In line with Japanese culture, every technique and method involves certain postures and stances with very precise actions and thoughts that are essential to the correct practice of each technique. Through the regular practice of these techniques the student will become more intuitive, more sensitive to the energy, be able to channel energy more effectively and strengthen their connection to the source of the energy. Other techniques are practiced as a form of self-healing. Again these techniques involve precise hand-positions and thoughts during the healing process.

Probably the biggest difference between Japanese and Western Reiki methods is a fundamental difference in the very core of the teachings. The Western approach in the main tends to be to teach simple techniques with little knowledge that are quick to learn and put into practice, without too much effort on the part of the students, or some of the teachers we have come across for that matter. With Usui Reiki Ryoho, the techniques are still simple, but every detail of every technique is much more precise and needs to be practiced until perfected. In line with Japanese culture, techniques are much more ritualised and almost ceremonial in their execution. There is a natural beauty to the Japanese techniques and the teachings have a natural feel to them.

There is now a great deal of interest amongst the Reiki community in the West, in the traditional Japanese form of Usui Reiki. This is partly to do with interest in the origins of Reiki and partly to do with the thirst for knowledge that is human nature. We have Reiki masters and writers travelling to Japan and meeting with any one that has any connection, however distant, to Reiki in this quest for knowledge. Books have been written and 'Japanese Reiki' workshops have proliferated. There is much good and valuable information available now about Japanese Reiki. But, there is also a great deal of misunderstanding and misinterpretation of the knowledge and practice of Japanese Reiki.

What is fundamental is to define the teachings and practices of Usui Reiki Ryoho and separate these from all the other Japanese Reiki techniques that have come out of Japan recently. Proclaiming something to be Japanese does not give it importance or relevance in the practice of Usui Reiki Ryoho.

The first thing that is important to remember is that Usui-sensei practiced and taught hands-on healing before his satori (initiation) and discovery of his Reiki. Some of the teachings of this earlier hands-on healing evolved and were adapted into his Reiki Ryoho, but some were not. His Reiki Ryoho itself changed with time as techniques were adapted and improved. We need to differentiate between the older hands on healing method and his later hands-on healing method if we are to truly understand and practice Usui Reiki Ryoho. Even more importantly we need to practice Reiki in the true spirit of Usui-sensei.

SECTION TWO
THE REIKI TRADITION

Chapter Twelve

Attunements and Reiju

The Attunement Process

The attunement process is an integral and essential part of Usui Reiki Ryoho. This is one aspect of Reiki that should have stayed constant and true to the original method without any changes or additions. Essentially, this is the primary method of connecting students to the source of the Reiki energy and is fundamental to the student's Reiki path.

There are many variations to the attunement process, which has been changed over the years through poor understanding, poor teaching or deliberate change by Reiki masters/teachers. Some of these adapted attunement methods work reasonably well, others are ineffective at best. We have had students trained elsewhere come on our courses and we have had to re-attune them because they did not have the connection to the Reiki energy, even though they were 'attuned' already.

A trained Reiki master/teacher performs a series of attunements on their students to provide or reinforce the connection between the student and the source of the energy. It makes no difference what you call the energy or where you believe it comes from.

The attunement process is really quite different to the traditional Reiju process. The traditional Reiju was a 'blessing' or 'empowerment' and was not used to connect the student to the source of the energy. Some Reiki teachers say that Reiju is simply the Japanese term for what is known in the West as attunements, but this is not strictly speaking true. The Reiju process itself has changed over the years, and various forms of Reiju are used by Reiki teachers around the world, some in the traditional context as a blessing, but others use Reiju in place of attunements. In the cases where Reiju is used as an alternative to attunements, the process will only be effective if the Reiju itself has been modified to make it similar to the attunements. We believe the attunement process is a later, more highly developed form of the original Reiju method that was developed by Usui-sensei to enable anyone to learn and practice his Reiki Ryoho in a short space of time.

The shirushi (symbols), jumon (name) and kotodama (mantra) are used in the attunement process to allow the students to connect to the universal vibrations or energy associated with them. Channels are opened and strengthened in the student to allow the energy to flow freely. The attunements raise the student's vibrational frequency so that they may become closer to the Universe or the source of the energy and hence become more aware.

The attunement process itself is taught to students at the master/teacher level in Reiki. The process is a precise set of actions with corresponding precise intentions. The process is ritualistic in nature, as are many other techniques in Japanese culture.

We have been informed by a relatively famous Reiki master/teacher that he believes attunements can be carried out any way a teacher wants and it will not matter, all that matters is the teacher's intention to attune a student. He went on to say he could attune students standing on his head in the corner of the room. There is so much wrong with this attitude that we hardly know where to start. Firstly as a Reiki teacher you should have enough respect for Usui-sensei's teachings to teach his method in his way. Secondly you should have enough respect for your students to teach them to the best of your ability. And finally you should have enough respect and love for Reiki to make sure your students are connected to the energy correctly and effectively for their own constructive self-development and practice.

Every action, every movement, every thought behind each action needs to be carried out accurately and with purpose and meaning. There are no short cuts or quick and easy options with the attunements. Every aspect of the attunement process has a specific and important purpose. As a Reiki teacher you need to respect the gift you are sharing with your students and carry out the attunements properly. You need to be focused and concentrate on what you are doing. Be in the moment and focus and concentrate on each stage as you are carrying it out.

The focus you learn from connecting to the energy when healing will help you when you are giving attunements. Again, as with healing, practice makes perfect, so practice as much as you can before you carry out attunements on students. You can practice with a cuddly toy or by visualising a person and attuning them.

The attunement process is the main difference between Reiki and other energy healing systems because it enables students to connect to, and channel, external energy from the Universe as soon as they are attuned. There is no need for many months or years of training, and because the energy is external to the practitioner, their own Ki is never used, so treating people with Reiki Ryoho is never tiring or energetically draining.

Some people are naturally connected to the Universe and can channel energy without being attuned, but most of these are only channelling energy in a passive way. Usui Reiki Ryoho allows you to heal conditions directly by using the shirushi, jumon and kotodama with colour to filter the energy to the frequency needed for any condition.

The attunement process is also a highly spiritual experience. For many students of Reiki, the attunements are the start of an amazing life-long spiritual journey of self-discovery and personal growth that gives ever-greater insights into their own path, and a far deeper understanding of the Universe. When you are attuned you are connected to the Universe or the Divine externally, and you are connected to the Universe or the Divine within too. This helps you to connect to your higher self, increasing your intuitive ability and guidance from the Universe. This in turn helps you find and follow your higher path if you choose to. The attunement process itself starts a healing process within you that heals you emotionally, physically and spiritually. It helps you to see life in a much clearer way and enables you to make healthier choices in your life and realise your true potential.

Reiju

Usui-sensei initially used Reiju in his teachings as he saw his students on a regular basis. Reiju is more an extension of Usui-sensei's earlier teachings, before his satori and discovery of his Reiki Ryoho. Students would attend classes weekly, some even daily, and Usui-sensei would raise their vibrational frequency in small steps as part of their on-going training. Reiju is taught at the master/teacher level in Reiki and is a ritualised process of specific actions and intentions through precise thought and energy transfer. As with attunements, the Reiju process needs to be carried out correctly to be effective.

Reiju empowerments do not give a direct connection to the source of the energy in the same way that attunements do, but put Universal energy into the student through the master/teacher, which raises their vibrational frequency. There are various methods of Reiju taught and practiced today, some use the shirushi as part of the process, many do not. Generally the shirushi are not used with Reiju. Over a period of time and with sufficient Reiju empowerments and self-development through Hatsu Rei-ho the students will reach the same level of connection and ability achieved through the attunement process. Reiju is actually a form of blessing, but is used as a form of minor attunement. Reiju needs to be given on a regular and ongoing basis to have the desired effect. Hatsu Rei-ho needs to be practiced every day at least once a day, though twice a day is preferable.

As Usui-sensei developed his Reiki Ryoho, the method he used to connect students to the source of the energy changed also. The attunement process was developed and used in place of the older from of Reiju. For students he would see less often, and for students learning Reiki on shorter courses Usui-sensei gave Reiju in a form that we would recognise today as attunements, which raise the students' vibrational frequency in very large steps. This later form of Reiju is what we believe Dr Hayashi used and taught to Mrs Takata. This is the basic form of the Western attunement process that was passed on from Mrs Takata.

Why Attunements Are Necessary

Usui-sensei said that he believed all life forms have healing power, with humans possessing the greatest healing power. The potential to use energy for healing purposes exists in all of us. All that is required for anyone to unlock their healing potential is a mechanism to allow them to channel, focus and direct the energy. For a very small number of people this is a natural process they go through without training or initiation, but for everyone else there needs to be some sort of deliberate conscious effort and training or practice involved. That is why Usui-sensei developed the Reiju and attunement processes to connect the student to the source of the energy. Together with the methods and knowledge of Usui-sensei's teachings the student can then develop their healing ability to their full potential.

The Benefits Of Attunements/Reiju Empowerments

Whichever method is used to connect the student to the source of the energy, the benefits to the student are the same. Once the student is connected to the source of the energy, a remarkable transformation takes place. The changes that come from this connection can sometimes be subtle and underlying and at other times they can be obvious and unmistakable.

Once attuned or connected to the energy, every Reiki student starts a wondrous journey of self-development and growth that brings about profound changes to every area of their life. The most obvious change is the ability to channel energy for healing. Through the attunement process the student is able to connect to and channel the different frequencies of energy that make up Reiki. With this energy they can work to treat any condition, illness or injury for themselves and for others, but Reiki has much more to offer than this. With the healing gift comes an increased awareness and heightened intuitive ability. An understanding and appreciation of one's own purpose and path becomes progressively discernible, making life flow smoothly and effortlessly. Choices and decisions are simpler and without conflict as the 'right' choice is always clear and indisputable. Life becomes a simple process of trusting your intuition and allowing life to be as it is and as it should be.

Chapter Thirteen

The Reiki Energies

The Shirushi Or Reiki Symbols

Shirushi is the traditional Japanese term for the Reiki symbols. Usui-sensei was presented with four symbols, the shirushi, in a vision during his satori (initiation), which came on the twenty-first day of the twenty-one day retreat he undertook on Mount Kurama in March of 1922. This is a part of the history of Reiki, which is disputed by some Reiki teachers. Some Reiki teachers believe Usui-sensei copied and adapted the shirushi (symbols) from existing Shinto or Buddhist rituals, some believe the symbols were Tibetan and others believe that the symbols are Japanese kanji that he modified.

We are unlikely to ever know with certainty how Usui-sensei discovered the shirushi, but we like to believe they were part of his satori on mount Kurama when he was given the gift of Reiki, as he has stated. However Usui-sensei discovered the symbols makes them no less effective or integral to Reiki. In traditional Japanese spiritual belief systems it is widely accepted that shapes have power, words carry spirit and sounds invoke universal vibrations or energy. This belief that shapes have power is the reason the shirushi are used in Reiki and this is the primary mechanism by which the shirushi work. The shirushi are not purely a means of focus or training wheels that can be discarded as the student becomes more proficient, but are integral and essential to the practice of Reiki.

Usui-sensei did not immediately use the shirushi as part of his Reiki Ryoho. He developed his Reiki Ryoho over a period of time, initially adapting his existing healing methods and techniques to work with his new discovery. As his knowledge and experience of Reiki grew his methods changed and he discarded some of his original methods and replaced them with his new system.

Part of his new system involved the use of the shirushi and their corresponding jumon (name) and kotodama (mantra) to connect to the energy. The other major change was the development of the Reiju empowerment process, which was changed to give instant connection to the source of the energy, now called the attunement process in the West. By this means any Reiki student once attuned could connect to and channel the correct energy to treat any condition.

Initially Usui-sensei taught students in a way similar to his martial arts teachings. Students would attend regular classes where they would learn techniques, which they would then practice until perfected. Once they had reached the required level of proficiency they would learn the next series of techniques and again practice until perfected....and so on, until they reached the top of the teachings.

Students would work on enhancing their energy flow by means of breathing exercises, meditation and stance/posture along with set moves.

Later Usui-sensei introduced Reiju whereby he would use energy to raise the students' vibrational frequency at every class. Initially there was no use of the shirushi or jumon or kotodama in this process. Students would learn to channel energy purely through focus and intention. This method took a long time to perfect and required a great deal of work and commitment by the students.

After his satori, Usui-sensei changed his teaching methods and eventually introduced the shirushi, jumon and kotodama into both the healing practice and the attunement process. This enabled students to become proficient as healers in a very short space of time and allowed them to channel universal energy at precise vibrational frequencies to work on any illness or injury.

It is believed Usui-sensei introduced the shirushi with their jumon and kotodama into his teachings in 1923. Using the shirushi effectively enabled students to heal physical and emotional conditions directly. Usui-sensei himself was able to do this without the use of the shirushi but he found that his students were not enlightened enough to be able to achieve this.

We will refer to the shirushi used in Usui Reiki Ryoho as CKR, SHK, HSZSN and DKM out of respect for Usui-sensei and to protect the use of shirushi. CKR was originally called shirushi 1, SHK shirushi 2, HSZSN shirushi 3 and DKM shirushi 4.

Each shirushi has its own jumon, that is a name or mantra that connects to the energy. Each jumon has its own kotodama that is a mantra or sound that connects to the energy. By using these three elements a Reiki practitioner can effectively connect to and channel Universal energy of specific vibrations or frequencies.

The mantras can be used independently of the symbols, and the symbols can be used independently of the mantras but they work best when used together, so they should always be used together.

The shirushi allow you to channel the correct frequency of energy for whatever condition you are treating, whether it is physical, emotional or spiritual. The jumon and kotodama used with the shirushi activate your connection to the Universal energy and also allow you to re-connect to the energy during the healing if at any point you lose your concentration and focus.

The geometry or shape and the colour of the shirushi dictate the frequency of energy you are using for each given healing. So you can see that the shirushi are vital components of the overall healing process. Without the shirushi you are generally either using your own Ki or life-force energy, or healing on a spiritual level with Rei energy, a high frequency energy described by Usui-sensei as light emanating from a practitioner's hands. With Rei you are not addressing any particular conditions or illnesses, which are usually manifested on a physical or emotional level.

Rei

Rei is one part of the Reiki energy and is commonly referred to as light or white light. Rei energy is a high frequency energy used to work on a spiritual or soul level. This energy works on the highest of your bodies, the spiritual body and is associated with your spiritual centre at the middle of your forehead. Healing with Rei will work primarily on a spiritual level, but as the three bodies are interconnected, there will be some minor effect on the emotional and physical bodies. Rei is the first energy you will learn to work with at the start of your Reiki path on level 1 courses.

CKR

CKR is one part of the Ki component of Reiki, and is also known as shirushi 1. CKR is used to connect and channel low frequency energy for healing the physical body. Changing the colour of the symbol changes the frequency allowing you to heal different physical and physical bordering emotional, conditions. This energy works on the lowest of your bodies, the physical body, and is associated with your physical centre at the tanden. Learning to work and self-heal with the CKR energy is the next stage of your Reiki path and is taught on level 2 courses.

SHK

SHK is the other part of the Ki component of Reiki, and is also known as shirushi 2. SHK is used to connect to and channel higher frequency energy for healing the emotional and mental body. The energy is a higher frequency range than from CKR and once again varying the colour can heal emotions of different frequencies ranging from traumas that are purely emotional to traumas that are almost on a physical as well as emotional level. This energy works on your middle body, your emotional body, and is associated with your heart centre. Learning to work and self-heal with the SHK energy is the next stage of your Reiki path and is taught on level 2 courses.

HSZSN

HSZSN is the 'Oneness' symbol, and is also known as shirushi 3. The HSZSN is not actually a healing symbol but a connection energy that is used to create oneness within and connections to others. HSZN is a fusion of Japanese Kanji rather than a healing symbol and can be translated as 'the core of yourself is right living.'

This shirushi is used to connect across space and time to anyone or anything including yourself. Once you have set the connection path you can send healing energy along the path. The HSZSN can be used for healing yourself or others distantly in the past, present or future.

When using HSZSN on yourself you are eventually able to create oneness by using this shirushi with CKR and then SHK to heal yourself on every level, physical, emotional and spiritual. When your mind, body and soul are balanced and in complete harmony, you achieve oneness and become in essence 'whole'.

The HSZSN energy is the bridge between your three energy bodies that connects and unites them as one.

Learning to work with the HSZSN energy is the next stage of your Reiki path and is taught on level 2 courses.

DKM

DKM is the 'Empowerment' symbol, and is also known as shirushi 4. In the West it is known as the Master symbol. The DKM is used in the attunement process and is given to students when they take a Reiki Master course. It is comprised of three kanji that translate as "Great Bright Light."

Being attuned to the master/teacher level with DKM dramatically raises your frequency, bringing you incredibly close to God or the Universe, making you more Divine or 'God like'. Through self-healing and 'right thinking and right living' you can develop and grow on a spiritual level and progress on your higher path until eventually you become enlightened. At this point you attain oneness with God, or the Universe. This energy connects you to God and is the bridge between Man and God, between Heaven and Earth. Learning to work with the DKM energy is the next stage of your Reiki path and is taught on level 3 (or 4) courses.

Taking a Reiki Master's course does not automatically make you enlightened though. Enlightenment comes from self-healing on every level until your frequency is so high that you can be close to God or the Universe. It also entails fulfilling your higher purpose for being here, taking responsibility for yourself and living in the best possible way for your soul's journey. This means that you are constantly listening to your intuition and always making the choices that are right for you.

When you are enlightened you become a passage between man and God, the bridge between Heaven and Earth. By teaching Reiki you are acting as a messenger, basically, you are working for 'God.' If you act against your intuition you cannot have a high frequency and be close to God. So for instance, if your intuition tells you that you must stop drinking alcohol on your path to enlightenment and you want to move further along your higher path you must follow your intuition. If you don't, then you cannot become enlightened.

Jumon

Jumon (*Lit. Japanese – spell or incantation*) is the Japanese term for the names of the shirushi and is used to mean 'words that carry spirit'. By saying the jumon you are connecting to the energy associated with the shirushi the jumon refers to. This is part of the philosophy of Japanese belief systems at the time of Usui-sensei. Usui-sensei taught students to connect to the Universal vibrations or energy through the use of jumon, kotodama and shirushi. By using these three methods any student of Reiki can connect to Universal energy of specific and precise frequencies, to work on any condition whether it is purely physical, emotional, spiritual or a combination of any of these.

Kotodama

Kotodama (*Lit. Japanese – jewelled words*) is a concept taken from both the Buddhist and Shinto belief systems. The use of kotodama is practiced by both faiths, and we are sure a similar concept exists in other faiths and religions around the world. kotodama is a very simple concept and was used by Usui-sensei in his Reiki teachings.

Kotodama comes from the belief that by making specific sounds with specific vibrations we can invoke specific universal vibrations or energies. By the use of kotodama we can connect to the Universe or the Divine both internally and externally. When used in the practice of Reiki, we can invoke specific universal vibrations or energies to treat physical, emotional and spiritual conditions directly.

The kotodama used in Usui Reiki correspond to the shirushi introduced by Usui-sensei. That is, each of the shirushi has its own corresponding kotodama, based on its jumon. The universal vibrations invoked by the shirushi and the jumon are the same as invoked by its kotodama.

Put simply, what this means is that a Reiki practitioner can connect to and channel specific frequencies of energy by using the shirushi and kotodama associated with those frequencies. When using kotodama the sounds need to come from deep within and must be slow and purposeful. Kotodama is used in sets of three and must be chanted rather than spoken, whether out loud or silently. The use of kotodama is integral and essential in the practice of Usui Reiki.

Connecting To The energy

Whenever you want to channel Reiki energy for any purpose you need to connect to the specific Universal vibrations or energy and stay connected for the entire length of time you are channelling. You need to ensure throughout the process that you are channelling energy externally rather than using your own Ki or life force. To connect to the specific Universal energy you use the relevant shirushi, jumon and kotodama. You can use the shirushi without the jumon and kotodama, as you can use the jumon and kotodama without the shrushi, but it is better to use them together to ensure the strongest possible connection and flow of energy.

How To Use The Shirushi And Their Jumon And Kotodama

There are various methods of connecting to the Reiki energy taught by different Reiki teachers, ranging from the very simple thinking or saying 'Reiki on,' to more elaborate and complex rituals involving affirmations, symbols, chanting, spirit guides and angels. Some even teach that all you need to do is put your hands on someone and think about healing them and the Reiki energy will start to flow immediately, and will intelligently treat whatever needs healing. Like a great deal of Reiki practice today, a simple and beautiful process has become mired in a mix of myth and Western or Eastern pseudo-spiritual add-ons.

The actual process of connecting to the Reiki energy is quite simple and beautiful, yet extremely effective when carried out properly.

The first step is to get into the correct frame of mind for healing. This is done through the use of the Gassho meditation. Gassho is used widely in the practice of Reiki and is a wonderful way to still, calm and focus the mind in preparation for healing or teaching or in any area of life that requires you to be in a relaxed, calm and focused state of stillness. Gassho means, 'bringing hands together' and is carried out as follows:

Bring your hands together in prayer position in front of your chest where your heart is. Close you eyes and empty your mind by concentrating on the tips of your middle fingers as they gently touch each other. If this is difficult to begin with, simply practice until it becomes easier. You can do this for anything from a few moments to 20-30 minutes.

You will find that the more you practice Gassho meditation the less time it takes to get your mind to the point of stillness and the focus this brings. Eventually you will find that as soon as your hands join in Gassho your mind stills immediately. This does of course take a great deal of practice. This is explained in greater detail in the next chapter.

Once you have stilled your mind, you can connect to the Reiki energy. This is done as follows:

Visualise or intend or simply have the feeling the relevant shirushi is above your head and either say the jumon or chant the kotodama (this can be silently or out loud) associated with the shirushi to make the connection and invoke the energy. You should use the jumon or kotodama in sets of three.

Visualise or intend or simply have the feeling that energy is flowing through the shirushi into the top of your head, down your neck, across your shoulders, along your arms and out of your hands. You should feel the energy in your hands at this point. The more you concentrate and focus the more you will feel the energy. Alternatively you can raise your arms above your head to form a v-shape and feel the energy travelling along your arms. Leave your hands in place until you can feel the energy strongly.

Stay focused on the energy coming from the shirushi to ensure you are never using your own Ki or life force energy. If your mind drifts away or you lose focus or concentration, gently bring it back with kotodama and visualisation or intention.

As you do this over many times you will find your mind learns to stay focused without too much effort. Practice does make perfect, so practice often to develop your concentration and focus. A still and focused mind will help you in many areas of your life, not just with your Reiki practice.

Kotodama can be used initially to connect to the energy or it can be used continuously throughout the process to help focus and concentration and to keep the connection to the universal vibrations or energy.

Chapter Fourteen

Traditional Usui Reiki Ryoho Methods

The methods used by Usui-sensei and his students are presented here for information purposes. Some of these methods and techniques are still taught by the Usui Reiki Ryoho Gakkai, some are still taught as part of some Japanese Reiki styles. Some are no longer taught or practiced.

Some of these older techniques involve stroking or tapping, which in some countries may require the practitioner to hold specific qualifications in areas other than Reiki. Please consult the legal requirements in your own country of practice before using any of these techniques.

For your own practice please stay within the law of your country and the guidelines of your governing body. It is your responsibility to work safely and lawfully.

Gassho

Gassho means literally to bring or press the palms together. This is a common posture in Japanese culture and is generally used to show respect and humility. When used in Reiki it becomes a point of focus and of unity and balance.

Gassho Meditation[4]

Gassho meditation builds on both the focus and unity and balance of Gassho. To carry out Gassho meditation, you sit in seiza with your eyes closed (you can use agura if you prefer) and bring your hands together in front of your chest where your heart is. Put your mind to where your two middle fingers meet at the tips of your fingers. Keep your mind focused on your middle fingers touching. If your mind drifts away, gently bring it back to your two middle fingers touching.

If any other thoughts come into your head, gently push them aside and go back to focusing on your two middle fingers touching. You may find this difficult at first, it does take a certain amount of training for the mind to focus and become still. The more you practice the easier it becomes and the quicker your mind stills and focuses. When you first start you may find it can take 20-30 minutes before your mind becomes still, but if you persevere and practice often you will find your mind becomes still virtually as soon as you put your hands in Gassho.

Postures And Sitting Positions

There are two common ways of sitting in traditional Japanese culture, formal and informal. The formal sitting posture is called seiza and the informal sitting posture is called agura.

When standing keep your feet shoulder width apart and your knees slightly bent. Your back should be straight and your weight should be centred and evenly distributed on both legs. Do not lean forward or back. Your shoulders should be relaxed.

To sit in Seiza you sit on the floor on your knees with your back straight. This can become quite painful after some time as many of us are not used to sitting in this way. It does take practice and determination to learn to sit in this way for long periods of time. Sitting in this way helps to develop your concentration.

To sit in Agura you sit on the floor with your legs crossed and your back straight. This is a more comfortable and perhaps relaxed way of sitting, and can be used in place of seiza in the practice of Reiki techniques.

You can place a blanket under your knees when sitting in seiza and a cushion may be used when sitting in agura for added comfort when you first start. As your joints and muscles become more flexible, you will start to perceive the benefits of this kind of sitting. If you find this too difficult, you can sit on a chair with your back straight.

Byosen Reikan Ho

Byosen Reikan Ho or scanning as it is called in Western Reiki, was taught by Usui-sensei in the early stages of a student's Reiki path.

Byosen Reikan Ho allows the practitioner to locate where on the client's body to place their hands to give the most effective healing by finding where there is illness or injury. This can be on any level, physical, emotional or spiritual.

The process itself consists of locating Byosen (*Lit. Japanese – source of the injury/illness*) by feeling for Hibiki (*Lit. Japanese – sensations felt in the hand*).

To carry out Byosen Reikan Ho:

Begin with Gassho to still your mind and bring your focus to the healing you are about to carry out.

The client stands with their eyes closed in front of you with their arms relaxed by their sides.

It is easier to use one hand for this technique. You should use the hand that energy flows out of more strongly.

Focus all your attention in the palm of your hand. Clear your mind of all other thoughts and distractions.

Start with your hand slightly away from the back of the client's head.

Slowly move your hand around the head and then continue around the whole body, keeping your hand the same distance away from the body.

Keep your mind focused on your hand and feel for any changes, such as heat or tingling or shaking or fluttering or cold or electrical sensations or a breeze. These are the hibiki. It does not matter how small the changes are, they indicate a need for healing.

Make a mental note of where the byosen are located. If you prefer you can write down the locations as you carry out Byosen Reikan Ho.

Once you have finished Byosen Reikan Ho you can either discuss what you have found with the client or simply treat the areas you found as you would normally, starting with the area where the strongest sensations were felt. We tend to discuss the byosen with the client to determine if they are physical or emotional conditions, as this will affect the way we treat each byosen. In this way we can give the most effective treatment.

End with Gassho to finish with gratitude and humility.

Enkaku Chiryo Ho

Distant healing method

This is something that is taught in some form on most Reiki level 2 courses. There are many variations on how to both connect, or more strictly speaking, choose the path the energy will travel along, and how to actually carry out the healing. The important elements are the correct use of the HSZSN in combination with either the CKR or the SHK.

Begin with Gassho to still your mind and bring your focus to the healing you are about to carry out.

Use the HSZSN and its jumon/kotodama to 'connect' to the person you will be sending healing to. Use visualisation and intention with the HSZSN to connect to the person.

Connect to the healing energy you will be using, either for physical, emotional or for spiritual healing. Use the relevant shirushi and its jumon/kotodama as you would for a normal hands-on healing.

Visualise the person you will be sending healing to and place your hands over the areas on the person that need treating, as you would for a normal hands-on healing.

End with Gassho to finish with gratitude and humility.

Gedoku Ho[4] (Also known as Tanden Chiryo Ho)

Method to detoxify and purify

This technique is used to remind your consciousness about your original nature (i.e. to help you connect to your higher self) through cleansing and purifying the body. The method is as follows:

Sit in seiza with your eyes closed and Gassho for a few minutes to focus and centre your mind. If you find it difficult to be centred you can do the Gassho meditation for a few moments.

Connect to the healing energy you will be using, either for physical, emotional or for spiritual healing. Use the relevant shirushi and its jumon/kotodama as you would for a normal hands-on healing.

Raise your hands above your head with your palms facing each other and feel the Reiki energy flowing down your arms.

Put your left hand on your forehead and your right hand on your tanden (3cms below your navel).

Keep your hands in this position for around five minutes.

Take your left hand from your forehead and place it over your right hand (on your tanden).

Keep your hands in this position for around twenty minutes.

End with Gassho to finish with gratitude and humility.

Hanshin Koketsu Ho[2] (also known as Ketsueki Kokan Ho)

Half body blood exchange

The client lies face down with their arms by their side.

Start at the top of the spine and work downwards unless the client has diabetes in which case you start at the base of the spine and work upwards.

Begin with Gassho to still your mind and bring your focus to the healing you are about to carry out.

Connect to the healing energy you will be using, either for physical, emotional or for spiritual healing. Use the relevant shirushi and its jumon/kotodama as you would for a normal hands-on healing.

Place your hands in the first position either at the top or the base of the spine. Your hands are placed palms down one either side of the spine with your fingers pointing up the spine (i.e. towards the head).

Sweep your hands gently and slowly to the side of the body.

Move your hands, one hand width down (or up if you are working upwards) and repeat the process.

Continue to do this until you reach the base of the spine (or the neck if you are working upwards).
Repeat this process 15 times.

Place your hands either side of the spine with your index and middle fingers gently pressed into the base of the neck. Breathe in deeply and hold your breath then gently and slowly move your hands down the spine and breathe out when you reach the bottom of the spine. Repeat 15 times.

Place your hands at the base of the brain and breathe in deeply and hold your breath. Gently and slowly move your hands down to the base of the spine then separate your hands and move them down the legs to the feet.

End with Gassho to finish with gratitude and humility.

Hatsu Rei Ho[3,5] (Shuyo Ho When Carried Out In A Group)

Strengthen spiritual energy method

Hatsu Rei Ho is an important and basic Usui Reiki Ryoho method. Hatsu Rei Ho is actually a series of individual techniques, all of which can be practiced separately. The process of Hatsu Rei Ho starts and ends with focusing your intent. A preparation to calm the mind is carried out before Hatsu Rei Ho is started. For students who receive initiation into Reiki through the attunement process, it is not an essential practice, but for students initiated through the Reiju process, Hatsu Rei Ho is essential and must be practiced daily. It is a combination of meditation, breathing exercise, and to a lesser extent minor empowerment and self-healing. Its practice enhances the flow of Reiki energy into you and through you and widens your 'energy channel' to enable you to connect to and channel energy more effectively. Hatsu Rei Ho should be carried out daily for between 30 - 60 minutes. This exercise was also carried out as a group activity (Shuyo Ho) by all the students and teachers during Usui-sensei's Reiki classes and Reiki meetings. There are a number of versions of Hatsu Rei Ho taught and practiced. This is one of these versions.

Preparation

Calming the mind

It is important to begin with relaxation in order to create a still and focused mind. In some Reiki traditions Hatsu Rei Ho begins with the chanting of Gyosei, the waka poems of the Meiji Emperor as a focus. With others, Gassho meditation is used.

Kihon Shisei

Standard posture

The standard posture for Hatsu Rei Ho is to sit in seiza.

Relax and slowly close your eyes.

Put your hands on your lap with the palms facing downwards.

Direct your attention onto your Tanden, approximately 3

centimetres below the navel.

Mokunen

Focusing

Silently say to yourself with meaning and purpose "I will start Hatsu Rei Ho now".

Kenyoku Ho

Healthy or dry bathing

This technique will cleanse your etheric and physical body and thus enable you to be a better channel for Reiki.

You should stand up for this technique.

Begin with Gassho to still your mind and bring your focus to the healing you are about to carry out.

Place your right hand, palm downwards, on the left shoulder so that the right fingertips are on the left shoulder (where the collar bone meets the shoulder). The hand is open and lying flat.

Breathe in deeply and as you slowly breathe out draw the hand down across the chest in a diagonal straight line, down to the right hip and just beyond. The hand stays palm down and either in light contact with the body or slightly above the body for the entire movement, to cleanse either the etheric or physical body.

Repeat this procedure on the right side, using the left hand, starting at the right shoulder and ending at the left hip and just beyond.

Repeat this procedure on the left side, using the right hand, starting at the left shoulder and ending at the right hip and just beyond.

Place the right hand again on the left shoulder, as above. Extend your left arm straight by your side, with the palm facing upwards. Breathe in deeply and as you slowly breathe out slide the right hand down the left arm all the way to the fingertips and just beyond.

Repeat this process on the right side, with the left hand on the shoulder and drawing it down the right arm to the fingertips and just beyond.

Repeat the process on the left side again, with the right hand on the shoulder and drawing it down the left arm to the fingertips and just beyond.

End with Gassho to finish with gratitude and humility.

Joshin Kokyu Ho

Purifying or Cleansing Breath

Sit in seiza. Place your hands on your lap with palms facing upwards and relax.

Inhale through your nose and exhale through your mouth. Connect to the Reiki energy as you would normally. As you inhale, breathe in the Reiki energy through the top of your head and into your Tanden, let your Tanden fill with Reiki energy.

Gently hold your breath (and the Reiki energy), for a few seconds. As you are doing this, imagine the Reiki energy flowing out of your Tanden and filling your entire being, let it flow into all of your body.

Exhale through your mouth. As you exhale, breathe out the Reiki energy through your body, through every part of you, so that the Reiki energy is flowing through you and out of you into the Universe.

Do this for a few minutes, or until you feel you have finished.

Gassho

Put your hands together in the Gassho position (prayer position), holding them in front of your chest by your heart.

Seishin Toitsu (also known as Gassho kokyu)

Unifying Spirit or contemplation

Remain in the Gassho position.

Inhale through your nose and exhale through your mouth. Connect to the Reiki energy as you would normally. While inhaling, breathe in the Reiki energy through your hands and along your arms and down into your Tanden. Let the Reiki energy fill your Tanden.

When you exhale, breathe the Reiki energy out of your Tanden along your arms and out of your hands.

Do this for a few minutes, or until you feel you have finished.

Gokai Sansho

Five Times Affirmations

Say out loud, with meaning and purpose the Gokai (Reiki Ideals or Precepts) three times. Take time to think about the words you are saying and what they really mean.

Mokunen

Focusing

Put your hands back on to your lap with your palms facing downwards.

Silently say to yourself, with meaning and purpose, "I have finished Hatsu Rei Ho now."

Heso Chiryo Ho²

Method for healing at the navel

This technique can be used for your self and others. It has particular healing effects for the kidneys. The method is as follows:

Sit in seiza with your eyes closed and Gassho for a few minutes to focus and centre your mind. If you find it difficult to be centred you can do the Gassho meditation for a few moments.

Connect to the healing energy you will be using, either for physical, emotional or for spiritual healing. Use the relevant shirushi and its jumon/kotodama as you would for a normal hands-on healing.

Raise your hands above your head with your palms facing each other and feel the Reiki energy flowing down your arms.

Place one hand over the navel with your middle finger either over or in your navel.

Place your other hand on the back directly behind the navel. This point is actually an acupuncture point that relates to the kidneys.

Keep your hands in place until you feel the body is in balance.

End with Gassho to finish with gratitude and humility.

Jakikiri Joka Ho

Jakikiri Joka-ho is a technique used to cleanse and purify. Jakikiri Joka-ho may also be used to break down large areas of negative energy to make them easier to treat. You would Jakikiri Joka Ho as part of a normal treatment rather than as a stand-alone technique.

To Use Jakikiri Joka Ho

Begin with Gassho to still your mind and bring your focus to the healing you are about to carry out.

Have the intention that you are cleansing and purifying or that you are breaking down negative energy.

Chop with the forearm three times over the area you are working on.

You can repeat Jakikiri Joka Ho a number of times until you feel the area is cleansed or the negative energy is broken down sufficiently.

End with Gassho to finish with gratitude and humility.

Nadete Chiryo Ho[2]

Stroking with hands method

Usui-sensei used stroking with the hands as part of his Reiki Ryoho. The stroking motion uses Reiki energy flowing from the hands to 'sweep' through the body. This can be to sweep negative energy out of the body or healing energy into the body. The hands can be just above the body or just brushing the body. Your intention to use the energy you are channelling to move energy within the client's body is vital to this method.

Generally you will use your dominant hand to stroke with.

Begin with Gassho to still your mind and bring your focus to the healing you are about to carry out.

Connect to the healing energy you will be using, either for physical, emotional or for spiritual healing. Use the relevant shirushi and its jumon/kotodama as you would for a normal hands-on healing.

The front and back needs to be treated.

For the back:

Start at the base of the neck, breathe in deeply and as you slowly breathe out, stroke down the centre of the back in one strong and slow movement and flick the energy away at the end. As you are doing this make sure you have the intention that you are 'sweeping' negative energy through the body and out of the body.

Repeat on the left side of the back.

Repeat on the right side of the back.

For the front:

Start with your hand at the heart area, breathe in deeply and as you slowly breathe out, stroke down the left side of the body and over the left leg to the toes in one strong and slow movement and flick the energy away at the end. As you are doing this make sure you have the intention that you are 'sweeping' negative energy through the body and out of the body.

Repeat on the right side of the body and the right leg.

Start with your hand at the heart area, breathe in deeply and as you slowly breathe out, stroke up the left side of the body to the left shoulder and along the left arm to the finger tips in one strong and slow movement and flick the energy away at the end. As you are doing this make sure that you have the intention that you are 'sweeping' negative energy through the body and out of the body.

Repeat on the right side of the body and the right arm.

For the head:

Use your index and middle fingers of both hands for the head area.

Start with your fingers at the point between the eyebrows and leave your fingers in position for a count of twenty-one as you intend the energy to flow from your fingertips. Breathe in deeply and as you slowly breathe out, stroke across both sides of the head horizontally until you reach the temples. Leave your fingers in position for a count of twenty-one as you intend the energy to flow from your fingertips.

Breathe in deeply and as you slowly breathe out, stroke across both sides of the head horizontally until you reach the ears in one strong and slow movement and flick the energy away at the end. As you are doing this make sure you have the intention that you are 'sweeping' negative energy through the body and out of the body.

Start with your fingers either side of the nose just below the eyes and leave your fingers in position for a count of twenty-one as you intend the energy to flow from your fingertips.

Breathe in deeply and as you slowly breathe out, stroke across both sides of the head horizontally until you reach the ears in one strong and slow movement and flick the energy away at the end. As you are doing this make sure you have the intention that you are 'sweeping' negative energy through the body and out of the body.

End with Gassho to finish with gratitude and humility.

Nentatsu Ho[2]

Method for attaining thoughts

This is a technique to help change negative patterns of thought or behaviour. The method is as follows:

Create your affirmation. It needs to be concise, positive and present tense.

Sit or lie in a comfortable position.

Close your eyes and Gassho for a few moments to focus and centre your mind. If you find it difficult to be centred, you can do the

Gassho meditation for a few moments.

Place one hand on your forehead.

Place the other hand on the back of your head over the base of the brain.

Repeat your affirmation out loud with purpose and belief for around five minutes (you can do this silently if your prefer).

Remove the hand from your forehead while keeping the other hand in place.

Relax for around five minutes.

End with Gassho to finish with gratitude and humility.

Oshite Chiryo Ho[2]

Pressing with hands method

Usui-sensei used the method of applying gentle pressure with the fingers as part of his Reiki Ryoho. This was used with the Reiki energy and was applied to specific conditions such as areas of stiffness or at the site energy blockages.

Begin with Gassho to still your mind and bring your focus to the healing you are about to carry out.

Connect to the healing energy you will be using, either for physical, emotional or for spiritual healing. Use the relevant shirushi and its jumon/kotodama as you would for a normal hands-on healing. Intend the energy to flow from your fingertips.

Apply gentle pressure with your fingertips at the area you are working on.

Repeat the process at any other area that requires it.

If you are doing this as part of a normal hands on treatment, continue the treatment.

End with Gassho to finish with gratitude and humility.

Reiji Ho[4]

Guided by intuition or spirit method

Sit in seiza with your eyes closed and bring your hands together in the Gassho position.

Do the Gassho meditation until your mind reaches a point of stillness.

Breathe in a controlled and calm manner.

Connect to the healing energy you will be using, either for physical, emotional or for spiritual healing. Use the relevant shirushi and its jumon/kotodama as you would for a normal hands-on healing.

Bring your hands back to Gassho in front of your chest at the heart area. Meditate on the healing you are about to give for a few moments.

Then, keeping your hands in the Gassho position, place them in front of your third eye. Pray for guidance so that your hands may be guided to where the Reiki energy is needed.

Trust in the guidance you are given, and detach from any thoughts of the outcome - simply let go of ego and allow the Reiki energy to flow through you.

Stand or sit by the client and place your dominant hand over the top of their head. Stay in a calm and meditative state through out the healing. Have no thoughts of the treatment, or the outcome or the effects of the healing.

Wait for guidance, in whatever form it comes to you - perhaps an impulse or an inspiration or a feeling, or even an inner knowing.

Move your hands as you are guided and allow the Reiki energy to flow without hindrance.

End with Gassho to finish with gratitude and humility.

Seiheki Chiryo Ho[2]

Method for emotional healing

Performed as Nentatsu Ho but the affirmation is replaced by the SHK kotodama

This is a technique to help change negative patterns of thought or behaviour. The method is as follows:

Sit or lie in a comfortable position.

Close your eyes and Gassho for a few moments to focus and centre your mind. If you find it difficult to be centred, you can do the Gassho meditation for a few moments.

Connect to the SHK energy as you would normally using the

shirushi, its jumon and kotodama..

Place one hand on your forehead.

Place the other hand on the back of your head over the base of the brain.

Silently or out loud chant the SHK kotodama for around five minutes.

Remove the hand from your forehead while keeping the other hand in place.

Relax for around five minutes.

End with Gassho to finish with gratitude and humility.

Uchite Chiryo Ho[2]

Patting with the hands method

You can use your finger tips, your fingers or the palms of your hands for this method. Which part of your hands you use will depend on the area you are working on. The smaller or more sensitive or delicate the area the lighter the patting should be and you should use the lighter parts of your hands such as the finger tips.

Always use very gentle pressure when you tap or pat with the hand. Use the wrist rather than the arm to ensure you are never putting any weight into the motion.

Begin with Gassho to still your mind and bring your focus to the healing you are about to carry out.

Connect to the healing energy you will be using, either for physical, emotional or for spiritual healing. Use the relevant shirushi and its jumon/kotodama as you would for a normal hands-on healing. Intend the energy to flow from your hands.

As you carry out this method have the intention that you are clearing negative energy from the body.

At the back:

Start at the top of the spine where the base of the neck is. Gently pat all the way down the spine to the base of the spine.

At the front:

Start with your hands at the heart area, breathe in deeply and as you slowly breathe out, gently pat down the centre of the body until you reach the pubic bone and flick away the negative energy.

Start with your hands at the area just below the collar bone, breathe in deeply and as you slowly breathe out, gently pat upwards and across to the shoulders and then along the arms to the hands and flick away the negative energy.

Start with your hands at the area just above the hip bone, breathe in deeply and as you slowly breathe out, gently pat downwards along the leg to the feet and flick away the negative energy.

End with Gassho to finish with gratitude and humility.

Zenshin koketsu ho[2]

Whole body blood exchange

Zenshin koketsu ho is carried out after a full body treatment. The client lies face down with their arms by their side.

Start at the top of the spine and work downwards unless the client has diabetes in which you start at the base of the spine and work upwards.

Begin with Gassho to still your mind and bring your focus to the healing you are about to carry out.

Connect to the healing energy you will be using, either for physical, emotional or for spiritual healing. Use the relevant shirushi and its jumon/kotodama as you would for a normal hands-on healing.

Place your hands in the first position either at the top or the base of the spine. Place your hands palms down, one either side of the spine with your fingers pointing up the spine (i.e. towards the head).

Sweep your hands gently and slowly to the side of the body.

Move your hands, one hand width down (or up if you are working upwards) and repeat the process.

Continue to do this until you reach the base of the spine (or the neck if you are working upwards).

Repeat this process 15 times.

Place your hands either side of the spine with your index and middle fingers gently pressed into the base of the neck. Breathe in deeply and hold your breath then gently and slowly move your hands down the spine and breathe out when you reach the bottom of the spine. Repeat 15 times.

Place your hands at the base of the brain and breathe in deeply and hold your breath. Gently and slowly move your hands down to the base of the spine then separate your hands and move them down the legs to the feet.

Place your hands at the top of the spine and breathe in deeply and hold your breath. Gently and slowly move your hands across to the shoulders and along the arms to the tips of the fingers. Repeat 15 times.

End with Gassho to finish with gratitude and humility.

Energy From The Eyes And The Breath

Usui-sensei taught that Reiki energy flows from the eyes and the mouth as well as the hands. When you are giving a treatment, you can maximise the effects of the healing by using Reiki energy from these parts of your body.

Gyoshi Ho

Healing through the eyes

This can be done during a hands-on healing to supplement the Reiki energy flow from the hands and/or the breath, or as a distinct healing on its own. The method is the same as you would use for healing through the hands.

Connect to the healing energy you will be using, either for physical, emotional or for spiritual healing. Use the relevant shirushi and its jumon/kotodama as you would for a normal hands-on healing.

Focus on the place you want to direct the Reiki energy, then relax the eyes and de-focus slightly.

Do not rely too much on your eyes; simply allow the energy to flow out of them.

Allow the energy to flow from your eyes to the point of healing like a river of energy.

Continue as you would for a hands-on healing.

Koki Ho

Healing through the breath

This can be done during a hands-on healing to supplement the Reiki energy flow from the hands and/or the eyes, or as a distinct healing on its own. The method is the same as you would use for healing through the hands.

Connect to the healing energy you will be using, either for physical, emotional or for spiritual healing. Use the relevant shirushi and its jumon/kotodama as you would for a normal hands-on healing.

Allow the energy to flow with your breath to the point of healing like a river of energy.

Continue as you would for a hands-on healing.

Chapter Fifteen

The Usui Reiki Ryoho Hikkei

The Usui Reiki Ryoho Hikkei is believed to be the companion handbook or manual for Usui-sensei's and Hayashi-sensei's Reiki courses. We have very kindly been given a copy of the Hikkei,[5] but we were unable to use it in this book. We wanted to have a translated copy printed in this section, but as this was not possible, we are explaining the Hikkei as best we can. The Hikkei is said to still be in use by the Gakkai. The Hikkei is divided into four sections. The first section is called 'Teachings of Usui Reiki Ryoho' and contains the Gokai (the Reiki ideals or precepts). The second section is called 'Explanation Of Instruction For The Public' and contains a series of questions about Reiki answered by Usui-sensei himself. The third section is called 'Ryoho Shishon' (Guide To Method Of Healing) and contains specific and detailed hand positions for treating many common minor and more serious illnesses. This was very much a beginner's guide for students to use early on in their Reiki Ryoho training. As students progressed they would develop sensitivity to the energy and would become more intuitive, so they would progress to more advanced techniques, such as Byosen Reikan Ho and Reiji Ho to locate the areas that needed treating.

The fourth section is called 'Meiji Tenno Gyosei' (Poems of the Meiji Emperor) and contains 125 waka poems written by the Meiji Emperor. It is believed the Meiji Emperor was a prolific writer of poetry and it is thought he composed many thousands of poems.

Section One: The Teachings of Usui Reiki Ryoho

The Teachings of Usui Reiki Ryoho is the first section of the Hikkei and is devoted to the Gokai, the Reiki precepts or ideals. This gives a good indication of the importance of the Gokai to Usui-sensei and to his Reiki Ryoho. There are a number of translations of the Gokai, due to the very nature of the Japanese language, which means the words can be interpreted in different ways. The meaning of the Gokai is pretty much the same for all the translations. For more detailed information about the Gokai see chapter 18.

Section Two: Explanation Of Instruction For The Public

The Explanation Of Instruction For The Public is a question and answer section in which Usui-sensei answers questions about his Reiki Ryoho.

The first part of this section is an introduction by Usui-sensei in which he explains why he wants his Reiki Ryoho to be shared freely and not kept within his family, as is the tradition in the Japanese culture of his era. He states that he believes society is in need of healing to promote peaceful and prosperous coexistence. Basically, people that learn Reiki or receive Reiki are happier, more content and get on easily with others. He goes on to say that his Reiki Ryoho is unique and is not something he was taught. He says that his Reiki Ryoho is an original system that is based on "intuitive power in the Universe."[5] It can be seen from the tone and content of Usui-sensei's introduction that he was an enlightened and evolved man. He was able to go against his upbringing and culture to give his teachings freely for the good of all, both individuals and society. He distinctly states that his Reiki Ryoho "is original... there is nothing like this in the world."[5] So, when modern Reiki experts say that Usui-sensei re-discovered Reiki they are disputing the founder of Reiki's own words.

The first question Usui-sensei is asked is what Reiki is. Usui-sensei explains that the first thing people have to do on their Reiki path is to heal their spirit, then they have to keep their body healthy. By healing their spirit, they can "achieve his teachings and training, improve physically and spiritually, and walk in a right path as a human being."[5] Usui-sensei defines the Usui Reiki Ryoho's mission statement as: "To lead peaceful and happy life, heal others and improve happiness of others and ourselves."[5] This is an interesting explanation of Reiki Ryoho. Usui-sensei talks about the fundamental elements of his Reiki Ryoho: healing yourself and living your life in the right way. The importance of self-healing and 'right thinking and right living' need to be remembered and practiced now as much as possible. He goes on to say that the first thing to heal is the spirit, hence on level 1 Reiki you learn to heal with the high frequency Rei or spiritual energy.

A very good question is asked next about Reiki's similarity to other forms of healing such as hypnotism and kiai method, and its similarity to religious practices. Usui-sensei replies emphatically that Reiki is not similar to these or any other forms of healing, nor is it a religious practice. He explains that his Reiki Ryoho uses 'intuitive power' to help the body and spirit, and that he gained this knowledge after many years of training. With this answer, Usui-sensei reinforces the fact that Usui Reiki Ryoho is both unique and is in no way similar to any other type of healing system. The fact that he feels his method is not religious should help those of a strict religious belief to accept Reiki.

This question follows from the previous one. Usui-sensei is asked whether Reiki is a spiritual method of treatment. Usui-sensei explains that Reiki energy is a form of psychic or spiritual healing, and that Reiki energy is also a physical form of healing. He explains that there are two types of energy used in his Reiki Ryoho; the light or spiritual energy and the Ki or life-force energy. He goes on to explain that Ki and Light emanate from the healer's body, primarily through the hands, eyes and mouth. He then describes the healing method using energy from the hands, eyes and mouth to treat the "affected areas such as... stomach ache, cuts, burns..."[5] He says that pain can be treated easily and quickly, but chronic diseases will take longer, but even after one treatment there will be an improvement. One of the most important elements of Reiki that has been lost is the direct healing element of Reiki. In this answer Usui-sensei says that injuries and illnesses can be treated with Reiki, that the pain of the illness or injury can be alleviated in one treatment and that the condition itself will take a number of treatments, but the condition should improve after just one treatment. According to Usui-sensei Reiki works on chronic and serious conditions, even though there is no medical explanation.

It is interesting that he refers to the fact that people need to actually see it to believe it, and that this cannot be denied or ignored even by people that use clever arguments and falsehoods to try to discredit it.

The question of whether a client has to believe in Reiki to get a better result is one that was asked of Usui-sensei, and is still asked by many clients today. Usui-sensei replies that Reiki is not like a psychological method of treatment that needs some level of belief to work, his Reiki Ryoho does not rely on the client believing in Reiki for the treatment to be effective. Reiki will work regardless of the client's belief, it will work whether the client accepts, denies or rejects it. Reiki does not rely on placebo or belief to work, nor is it a psychosomatic effect, so it does not matter whether the client believes in Reiki, or whether they are a total skeptic, the effectiveness of the treatment will be the same. He says that there are maybe one in ten clients that believe in Reiki before receiving a treatment, but that most believe in Reiki after they have felt the benefits of a treatment. Then, like now, most people will not believe in Reiki until they have a treatment and experience the healing benefits. The other thing to take from this paragraph is the fact that a client cannot deny or block the healing energy. Too many Reiki therapists now will say, "The reason the client did not get better was because they rejected the energy" rather than look at the quality of the treatment they gave.

Usui-sensei is asked if his Reiki Ryoho can cure any illness. He replies that any illness can be cured by his Reiki Ryoho, such as psychological or organic illnesses. This is such an important statement: "any illness... can be cured by this method." [5] How has this been lost over the years? Today so many Reiki practitioners and teachers say that Reiki does not treat conditions nor does it heal or cure anything. By their ignorance they have reduced the Great Reiki of the Universe, the 'miraculous medicine of all diseases' to the realms of a relaxation therapy.

The follow-on question of does Usui Reiki Ryoho only heal illness is asked next. Usui-sensei replies that Usui Reiki Ryoho does not only heal physical illnesses, it heals mental and emotional illnesses. He refers to agony, weakness, timidity, irresolution, nervousness and other bad habits, which can be corrected with Reiki treatments. We would understand these types of illnesses today as emotional and behavioral problems. Once healed on all levels, people will be able to lead happy and fulfilled lives. By doing this we can become closer to our true spiritual nature and live our lives in a more Divine way, which in turn allows us to heal others with "mind of God (or the Universe) or Buddha" [5]

When asked how Usui Reiki Ryoho works, he states that he was not given this method by anybody nor did he study to get this psychic power to heal. He goes on to say that he realized he had received healing power when he felt the 'air in a mysterious way' during fasting (the retreat he undertook on Mt Kurama). He says that even though he is the founder of Usui Reiki Ryoho, he cannot explain exactly how it works, but he believes that in the future science will have an explanation. .

The question of whether Usui Reiki Ryoho uses any medicine and if there are any side effects is asked. Usui-sensei replies that Reiki Ryoho does not use any medical equipment, and the method of treatment is through the use of energy. The energy is applied to the affected area by staring at it, breathing onto it, stroking with the hands, laying on of hands and patting lightly with hands.

Usui-sensei is asked whether Reiki practitioners need to have medical knowledge to practice Reiki. Usui-sensei replies that his Reiki Ryoho is beyond a 'modern science' and does not require any knowledge of medicine. He says that if "brain disease occurs, I treat a head. If it's a stomachache, I treat a stomach. If it's an eye disease, I treat eyes."[5] Usui-sensei states very clearly and categorically here that he puts energy at the affected or damaged area by the various methods he described earlier. He states a treatment need only be for a short time yet the condition will improve when working in this way, and that this is why his Reiki Ryoho is "very original." [5] No where does Usui-sensei say "the energy will go where it needs to", yet today so many Reiki experts preach that "the energy is intelligent and goes where it needs to," so you do not have put the energy in any place in particular nor do you need to think about what to treat on any client, the energy will know what to treat and simply go there and treat it. This is so far removed from the original purpose of Reiki that we find it astounding that so many within the Reiki community work in this way.

The opinions about Reiki of famous medical scientists are asked in this question. Usui-sensei explains that generally, European scientists are critical, whereas the Japanese scientists are more reasonable. He goes on to quote a number of doctors and scientists such as Dr. Nagai of Teikoku Medical University who says, "we as doctors do diagnose, record and comprehend illnesses but we don't know how to treat them."[5] Dr. Kuga says, "it is a fact that psychological therapy and other kind of healing treatment done by healers without doctor's training works better than doctors, depending on type of illnesses or patient's personality or application of treatment." [5]

The opinion of the medical profession is important to the acceptance of Reiki within the wider community. It can be seen from this paragraph that Usui-sensei was keen to show his students that his Reiki Ryoho was a valid healing system respected by the medical profession.

He goes on to say that doctors, medical scientists and pharmacists once they see the effectiveness of Reiki Ryoho they actually learn the method for themselves. It is a sign of Reiki's acceptance at the time that doctors, medical scientists and pharmacists decided to learn Reiki with Usui-sensei. Scientists are by nature inquisitive and will generally accept a theory as fact based on empirical evidence, so this speaks volumes about the effectiveness of Reiki as taught by Usui-sensei.

This question is one of regulation and the law. Usui-sensei is asked what the government's reaction is to Reiki Ryoho. The reason for this question is the fact that a member of the Diet (Parliament) Dr. Matsushita, raised the question of people without any medical doctor's training treating many patients with psychological or spiritual methods of treatment. Mr. Ushio, a government delegate replied: "a little over 10 years ago people thought hypnosis is a work of long-nosed goblin but nowadays study has been done and it's applied to mentally ill patients. It is very difficult to solve human intellect with just science. Doctors follow the instruction how to treat patients by medical science, but it's not a medical treatment such as electric therapy or just touching with hands to all illnesses."[5]

Basically, as Usui Reiki Ryoho is not classed as a medical

treatment, it does not violate the Medical Practitioners Law or Shin-Kyu (acupuncture and moxa treatment) Management Regulation.

This question is one asked by many new students. Does a student have to have a special gift or ability to be able to practice Reiki? Usui-sensei replied that all life forms have a form of healing power, but humans have the most developed or in his words "remarkable (healing) power."[5] He says that Usui Reiki Ryoho utilizes and materializes the healing power that humans have.

This is gives a huge insight into Usui-sensei's Reiki Ryoho, the fact that Usui-sensei believes every life form has healing power, with human beings having the greatest healing ability. What Usui-sensei was given during his satori was the knowledge and ability to realize any and every one's healing potential through initiation and training in his Reiki Ryoho. Basically anyone can be initiated into Reiki and give effective healing treatments through the teachings of Usui-sensei.

This is a good question, one, we routinely get asked as Reiki teachers. Can anyone be initiated into the art of Reiki? The answer then, as now, is anyone can be initiated into Reiki. There is no need for any prior knowledge, or ability, all that is required, is the desire to learn and common sense. Anyone, regardless of their age or sex, as long as they have common sense, can be given the power in a short time enabling them to heal both themselves and others. He explains that it is a characteristic feature of his Reiki Ryoho to be able to heal difficult illnesses easily and quickly.

This is a question we often get asked too, which demonstrates how little things have changed over the years. The interviewer asks if he can use Reiki Ryoho to heal himself, to which Usui-sensei replies that if he can't heal himself, how can he heal others? It seems an obvious answer really, but many students ask the same question now. Reiki starts with self-healing and ends with self-healing. Self-healing is an essential part of any Reiki student's path. Usui-sensei is asked how a student can receive the Okuden level. He replies that he would only accept students onto the higher levels of his teachings if they were enthusiastic and demonstrated commitment to his teachings and lived their lives in the appropriate way for Reiki students, that is with 'right thinking and right living'. He goes on to detail some of the Okuden techniques, such as Hatsu Rei Ho, patting with hands, stroking with hands, pressing with hands, telesthetic (distant healing) and propensity (use of intention) methods.

The final question is whether there is a level higher than Okuden. Usui-sensei explains the level after Okuden is called Shinpiden.

Section Three: Ryoho Shishon

The Ryoho Shishon or 'guide to method of healing' is a Reiki practitioner's guide to directly and effectively treating illnesses and injuries with specific hand positions for each condition. The Ryoho Shishon is sub-divided into eleven sections, each section covering specific body areas and illnesses. The sections of the Ryoho Shishon are:

Section 1. Basic treatment of body parts
Section 2. Nerve diseases
Section 3. Respiratory diseases
Section 4. Digestive System Diseases
Section 5. Circulatory/Cardiovascular Diseases
Section 6. Metabolic And Blood Diseases
Section 7. Urinary Diseases
Section 8. Surgical And Dermatological Diseases
Section 9. Pediatric Diseases
Section 10. Gynecological Diseases

Section 11. Contagious Diseases

This healing guide was intended for new students to use to help them treat clients for the majority of known illnesses and injuries at the time. You can see from the list of sections how comprehensive the Ryoho Shishon is. The purpose of it is to allow students to very quickly treat clients, even ones with serious illnesses. The methods and hand positions are precise and specific, unlike some of the modern Western Reiki systems that teach the energy is intelligent and will go where it is needed. As students develop a deeper understanding and sensitivity to the energy, they will be able to use their intuitive ability along with the more advanced Reiki Ryoho methods.

The Ryoho Shishon gives a very clear insight into Reiki as a healing therapy. It is obvious from this that Reiki was traditionally taught as a healing therapy, and practitioners treated illnesses and injuries directly. Reiki was never intended to be used as a 'relaxation' therapy. Reiki was and is an amazing healing system.

Section Four: Meiji Tenno Gyosei

The final section of the Usui Reiki Hikkei is dedicated to the waka poems of the Meiji Emperor. The Meiji era was known as the 'Enlightened Rule' during which Japan developed and grew in power to emerge as the dominant force in the Pacific. The emperor, Mutsuhito, was believed to have been a spiritual man, some even go as far as to say he was a pacifist at heart. He is credited with writing many thousands of poems, a small selection of which are included in the Hikkei.

Chapter Sixteen

Why We Must Remember Usui-sensei

Reiki as we know it now has been changed so dramatically by so many people around the world that the more traditional form is becoming increasingly hard to find. Many forms of Reiki now in existence are not really Reiki Ryoho (as Usui-sensei taught) at all. We have heard so many practitioners and teachers saying that what Usui-sensei taught is not really important anymore and neither is the history or tradition of Reiki. Some Reiki teachers have the opinion that it does not matter what they teach or how they teach it, Reiki is simply a case of putting your hands on the person and allowing the energy to flow.

There are Reiki teachers that believe Reiki is constantly evolving and it is only natural that they make changes and additions to Usui-sensei's system of healing. After all they are improving the original, in their view anyway. This is a complete travesty and goes against the traditions and belief system on which Reiki was founded. Usui-sensei discovered and developed his Reiki Ryoho and it was expected of his students to honour him as their teacher by following his teachings and keeping his teachings as they were given to them. The knowledge of the great Reiki of the Universe was bestowed upon Usui-sensei through his endeavour and effort in self-development and spiritual growth. He was chosen above billions of people around the world to receive the satori (enlightenment) and the ability to heal any condition – physical, emotional or spiritual with this gift. Anyone can develop their own particular system for channelling energy for healing purposes, but it will not be Usui Reiki Ryoho. The system founded by Usui-sensei is a wonderful method that anyone can learn and use for their own and other's benefit. The teachings of Usui-sensei are a complete system that has to include all of the techniques and knowledge of his Reiki Ryoho. Usui-sensei was tasked with spreading this gift to as many people as he could and spent his whole life dedicated to improving his mind, body and spirit and helping others to do the same. We owe it to Usui-sensei, to ourselves and to our clients and students to practice and teach Reiki the way Usui-sensei did and to have respect for the founder of this system of healing.

There are plenty of people now that claim they have channelled new symbols or new energies from the Earth, the moon, the sun, Mars, crystals, animals, trees, mythical creatures, there is now even Sex Reiki and Money Reiki...the list is almost endless. The primary point that all these people are missing is that Reiki is a complete form of healing in itself. Reiki uses energy from God or the Universe and contains all the frequencies needed for every condition that could ever possibly exist. Why would we need any other healing energies?

The danger is that by forgetting where Reiki came from we actually forget what it was for in the first place. Too many people now see Reiki as a badge to wear and treat the energy in a frivolous way, as a new toy to show to their friends.

We have heard about many Reiki practitioners who use Reiki flippantly, to try to change the traffic lights, get a parking space and improve the taste of wine, to name but a few. Usui-sensei was a very serious man, he did not suffer fools gladly and it is up to us to be serious about our Reiki work and to treat the energy with the utmost respect. Usui-sensei set us all a very important example, one that we should all strive to follow if we want to be good Reiki practitioners and teachers.

SECTION THREE
REIKI THE SPRITUAL PATH

Chapter Seventeen

The Spiritual Nature of Reiki

Reiki is by its very nature and practice, a spiritual healing method. Reiki does not need to be taught or practiced in a spiritual way, there does not need to be any belief system in place for a student to learn Reiki, nor does there need to be any belief system in place to receive effective Reiki treatment.

This may sound like a paradoxical statement, but it is a fact. Anyone can use Reiki regardless of their beliefs or faith as long as they are attuned and they connect to the energy in the appropriate way. Anyone can receive Reiki treatments and the energy will be equally as effective regardless of the receiver's beliefs or faith - Reiki cannot be 'blocked' by the receiver as is commonly believed - the energy will work on whatever is being treated.

Reiki was discovered by Usui-sensei, an enlightened and spiritually advanced man during a twenty-one day spiritual practice. The essence of Reiki is the connection between the practitioner and the source of the energy. This connection is the spiritual nature of Reiki. By choosing to connect oneself to the source of the energy one becomes open to the Universe or God or whatever term fits with ones own culture and beliefs/faith.

Taking The Spiritual Path – Reiki Is A Lifestyle Issue

No matter how Usui Reiki Ryoho is taught or practiced, it is a spiritual path first and foremost. You will find different people will have their own 'take' on what this means and how it fits in with their lifestyle.

This is an aspect of Reiki and of life that causes much debate. It is in fact very simple, but yet there are many interpretations. We have heard Reiki Masters say that they can live a physical life and a spiritual life at the same time, that being spiritual does not mean they have to give anything up. We have even heard of Reiki masters that are happy to take drugs and alcohol and still proclaim their spiritual credentials.

There can be no argument about this issue. There is no such thing as a spiritual life that is physical too. This may be true at the beginning of a spiritual journey, but becomes less so as the journey unfolds. Continued spiritual growth entails a change of priorities and an alteration in the way of living. The further you want to travel on your spiritual journey the greater the changes you will experience. It is up to you how far you travel along this path and it is up to you how much you allow yourself to change.

Just remember to be honest with yourself and accept yourself wherever you are on your path. This is a personal journey of spiritual growth, which is unique to every individual. Be proud of every step you take on your journey. Be proud of the first step you take, even if it is the only step you take. Do not compare yourself to others and their path and do not try to compete with others. It is not a competition to see who can be the most spiritual.

When a student is initiated into the Reiki path, the process of attunement raises their spiritual vibrational frequency and starts their spiritual journey. As they self-heal their frequency raises further. By raising their spiritual frequency they are in effect becoming more Divine in their nature and outlook. This leads to greater awareness and insight. With greater insight comes knowledge and with knowledge comes change. The irony is that the more you know the less you can do, but, the more you know the less you want to do. This sounds like a paradox, but it is a simple truth.

This has an effect on their physical and emotional life also. As anyone progresses on their spiritual journey they will naturally distance themselves from their physical life. As a crude example, it may be acceptable to drink copious amounts of alcohol when living a physical life because this seems the 'norm' and fits in with the level of awareness at this time. But as awareness increases through self-healing, one will soon realise that drinking alcohol hinders one's spiritual growth. The choice is then with you whether you want to continue your spiritual growth and reduce (or stop) your alcohol consumption or carry on drinking alcohol and stall (or even reverse) your growth.

The choice is always with you. The extent to which you travel along this spiritual path is not dependent on how much you want this to happen but on how much effort you put into your spiritual growth. Only by putting time and effort into raising your frequency and accepting and embracing the changes that come along the way can you progress spiritually.

This is a fundamental fact that cannot be argued away. Every one has choices in life that dictate their path. No one can follow two paths.

Following a spiritual path is not easy, nor is it meant to be. We are all spiritual beings in a physical body in a physical world. We need to find the balance between our spiritual and physical lives that fits in with our level of awareness at any given moment and be prepared to change our lives as our awareness changes.

Chapter Eighteen

The Gokai

The Gokai or Reiki precepts or Ideals are an essential part of Usui Reiki Ryoho, and need to be understood and followed as part of any Reiki path.

The Gokai were developed by Usui-sensei and taught to his Reiki Ryoho students to help them develop a pure and sound mind and to encourage, as he called it, 'right thinking and right living'. The Gokai were used to meditate on and chant at every Reiki Ryoho class or meeting. Students were also expected to do this in their daily lives as part of their spiritual growth and development.

There are various versions of the Gokai being taught, some are variations of the Reiki ideals presented by Mrs Takata. The others are various translations of the original Gokai taught by Usui-sensei.

As Presented By Mrs Takata

Just for today, I will let go of anger.
Just for today, I will let go of worry.
Just for today, I will give thanks for my many blessings.
Just for today, I will do my work honestly.
Just for today, I will be kind to my neighbour and every living thing.

A Translation Of The Usui Reiki Ryoho Gokai[3]

The secret method of inviting happiness
The miraculous medicine of all diseases
Just for today, do not anger

Do not worry and be filled with gratitude
Devote yourself to your work and be kind to people
Every morning and evening join your hands in prayer, pray
these words to your heart and chant these words with
your mouth
Usui Reiki Treatment for the improvement of body and mind
The founder
Usui Mikao

(The *middle section* are the Gokai)

Living The Gokai

As a Reiki healer you need to take the Reiki precepts to heart and fully understand and apply them to yourself to attain enlightenment. The precepts all have a deeper meaning, which needs to be meditated on.

Usui-sensei developed these precepts to complement the five stages to complete our spiritual circle of life, beginning with the re-awakening of our true spiritual nature when we first learn Reiki and culminating in enlightenment when we become a true Reiki Master. After this we return to spirit as we die from this world and return to the source of the energy or God or the Universe.

Usui-sensei called Reiki the "Secret method of inviting happiness, the miraculous medicine of all diseases." Reiki really does have the ability to bring happiness to your life if you practice this healing system as it was originally intended. There are no limits to what Reiki can do, other than those you place on yourself.

Below you can find the deeper meaning of the precepts and how they apply to your every day life. The precepts in brackets are referring to Takata's version.

Just For Today

Just for today sets you in the present tense so that you are thinking in a conscious aware manner and not placing unreasonable demands on yourself. By setting your precepts in the present you are establishing achievable goals for yourself and not worrying about yesterday or the next day, today is what is important, the here and now. As you build on each day it becomes easier to fulfil the precepts indefinitely.

Do Not Anger (I Will Let Go Of Anger)

Letting go of anger is important for you to be at peace with yourself and others. This does not mean that you will never get angry about anything, nor does it mean that you should never get angry. Events take place in the world every second of the day that *should* make everyone angry. There are atrocities and there is ignorance in the world and if this goes against your ethics it is bound to make you feel aggrieved.

However you need to learn **how** to channel that anger and also accept that there are things that you cannot change. Focus on the areas where you can make a difference, rather than dwelling on the areas where you cannot. There is no use sending healing to the third world or to natural disasters. People in the third world need other human beings who are in government to make drastic changes for their lives to improve. If you want to help those in the poorest nations, you would be better off going to work for a charitable organisation such as Christian Aid, than sending prayers or healing.

A natural disaster can be a warning signal to humans, to prompt awareness of the damage they have done to the world. We cannot change these things with healing but we can accept that they occur and make a difference to the people around us and as healers to the clients that come to us. We can educate people and additionally we can change our own lives, for example: by becoming vegan, by altering our purchasing patterns and switching to more ethical and organic products, by always trusting in our intuition and never deviating from its guidance. The latter suggestion is the only route to happiness and continued fulfilment. The other two often form part of our abidance to our intuition.

As your awareness increases you will foster a greater understanding of your own anger and with dedication to your spiritual growth, you will eventually start to see the world and yourself in a much healthier light. It is true that the truth is often disturbing, but it will also liberate you and help you to understand yourself and the Universe more completely.

Do Not Worry (I Will Let Go Of Worry)

We all worry far too much for our own good. Some people worry about everything: waking up on time, getting to work on time, high achieving at work, taking the children to school, what people think of them. When you learn Reiki and become more aware, taking the precepts to heart, you develop a greater awareness of yourself and the Universe. With this newfound awareness you gain a whole new perspective on what is really important in life. You learn to see people as they really are and the things that used to make you feel stressed on a day-to-day basis, no longer seem so important and overwhelming. Rather than being tangled inside the stresses of life you become more of a detached outsider, with a more objective viewpoint.

Being detached is essential to our well-being. It does not mean that we don't care about anyone or anything. Rather it means that we are able to perceive everything from a much higher, more Divine perspective. We love unconditionally and this inherently means being honest to ourselves and to others. As a result, we become less concerned about what others think of us, and more concerned about pursuing our higher paths on Earth and listening to God or the Universe and our intuition. This alleviates a great deal of our worry, because we alleviate the pressure of pleasing others and instead focus on nurturing our souls.

Obviously it is difficult to banish worry completely. Even if you are perfectly happy within yourself, there are always external stressors in life, such as: relationships with other people, money worries and health issues. However, as you self-heal and heal others you learn to re-prioritise your life and develop a faith that no matter what happens to you, everything will be as it should. This helps you to get past the constant worrying and makes you emotionally stronger as a person.

Be Filled With Gratitude (I Will Give Thanks For My Many Blessings)

Giving thanks for all your blessings means being grateful for everything that has happened to you in your life, whether you regard any of those events as good or bad. This is perhaps the hardest precept of all to live by, but once you come to accept your pain as a blessing, as much a blessing as your joy, your spiritual growth soars dramatically. It is not enough just to say the right words; you have to truly be thankful for everything.

Most of the experiences we go through in life teach us or someone else a valuable lesson. The whole point of life is to learn from the lessons we are given, if we do not learn, we will continue to go through the same experiences over and over again. We learn from our mistakes and from the mistakes of those around us. It can be exceedingly hard to perceive something as a blessing when it seems to cause us so much anguish. Often it is easier for us to blame someone else or blame God, but ultimately we have to take responsibility for our own decisions in life.

Once you finally learn to accept the pain as well as the joy, you become a much more balanced and content person, with better coping mechanisms.

Devote Yourself To Your Work (I Will Do My Work Honestly)

This precept is primarily referring to your spiritual work not your 'nine-to-five' job. Of course we should all be honest in every area of our lives but completing our spiritual work is the most important task we have to do. We all come to Earth with a higher path to follow and travelling along that path should be the main priority in our lives. Other aspects of being here on Earth tend to fall into place once you are committed to fulfilling your higher purpose.

When you are on your higher path you need to strive to stay on that path, always trust your intuition and work with honesty. If you come off your higher path at any stage it is very difficult to get back on it again, and that is assuming you are able to return to your higher path.

And Be Kind To People (I Will Be Kind To My Neighbour And Every Living Thing)

To achieve enlightenment we need to love every living thing unconditionally. This concept seems to confuse some people. It does not mean that we have to be excessively amiable to everyone. Declaring that we love someone unconditionally does not mean that we have to like that person. Sometimes to teach someone a lesson we have to be direct and honest and say things to them that they may not want to hear.

We need to be honest with each other and loving others unconditionally means that we are prepared to share some harsh home truths, to stand back from situations when necessary, even if we are asked for help, because in that instance, by doing nothing we are helping in the best possible way. It's about doing what is right for someone's soul, over and above their physical body. This could mean causing upset in the short term, for long term spiritual gain.

A pre-requisite of loving unconditionally is being more detached from people so that we are not dependent on others for our own well-being. It is of no advantage to anyone if we spend all our time trying to please others. We are all here to fulfil our higher purpose and that is where we should be concentrating all of our efforts.

We have heard it said that there are no bad humans only bad human actions. This is not true; there are people that are in a human sense, 'bad.' However, what we may consider to be a bad action is seen quite differently on a universal scale, because everyone has a purpose for being here. It is simply the case that some people are here to deliberately cause harm, in order to teach others lessons about their own behaviour, or to take them off their path in life.

Avoid people that set out to do you harm. If you come across someone who says all the right things but make you cringe, then your intuition is telling you that there is something very negative about this person. That uncomfortable feeling you are getting is a warning signal.

We really don't have to like everyone or be nice to everyone. If we feel that someone is bad or we simply don't get on with them, our best option is to avoid being in their company. There is no point getting drawn into conversations with people who will ultimately make you feel very negative and draw you away from what you should be doing.

If you have to converse with someone you do not like because of a work commitment then find a way of dealing with that person that offers minimal contact. When you do have to communicate with them be direct and assertive, to make them aware that you are not going to take any nonsense from them. By doing this they will not be able to steal your energy or drag you away from your higher purpose.

Being kind to every living thing of course includes animals and other creatures. To be truly enlightened you cannot eat meat or any animal products, because to do so you would be consenting to unnecessary harm being inflicted upon living creatures. It does not mean you are a bad person if you eat animal products, it simply means that you cannot attain enlightenment. Eating animal products lowers your frequency as you are consuming a creature that has suffered for your pleasure.

In the West we have no excuse to eat meat. There are plenty of other cheap and more nutritious protein sources available. Animals now are often kept in factory farms, they are abused, tortured and die a horrible painful death, not to mention the antibiotics that are pumped into them along with other harmful substances. The stress the animal experienced and the detrimental substances the animal was fed are then absorbed into our own bodies. Once you become enlightened, to eat meat would take you off your higher path.

Every Morning And Evening Join Your Hands In Prayer, Pray These Words To Your Heart And Chant These Words With Your Mouth

By joining your hands in prayer (gassho in Japanese) you are showing respect for God, yourself and all living things. You are creating 'oneness' within yourself and with the Universe, uniting body, mind and soul. By praying the precepts to your heart you are committing to live by the precepts.

Chanting the five precepts out loud allows you to voice the commitment you have made to follow all these guidelines, planting them firmly in your conscious as well as subconscious, mind.

The whole action involved with this precept combines the physical (gassho), spiritual (prayer) and psychological (chanting) to reinforce the accomplishment of all the five precepts within your whole being.

Chapter Nineteen

Trusting Your Intuition

Trusting our intuition is one of the most important, and we would even go so far as to say, essential lessons we need to learn in life. Allowing our intuition to guide us will ensure we make the best possible choices at any given time. Our intuition is not limited by our knowledge, nor is it conditioned by our upbringing or environment. Our intuition has all our answers and is not affected by our thoughts, our emotions, our friends or our family. Our intuition is our higher self, our spiritual self, talking to us, which is the part of us that communicates with God or the Universe. Our higher self is the bridge between the human and the Divine, the physical and the spiritual, Earth and Heaven. Our higher self is that which is Divine, which exists within all of us. Our intuition is our guide that is always right, that leads us along our higher path to God or the Universe.

This all sounds great, but just how easy (or hard.) is it to trust our intuition? Well, lets start with what guides us generally.

We all have to make choices in our lives, from the seemingly very trivial that have little immediate impact on our lives to the very important that can change our lives instantly. All decisions affect our lives, whether the impact is immediate, long-term, obvious or imperceptible. By what mechanism do we make these decisions? We can think of a number of processes we go through to make a decision, such as:

❖ Looking at the outcome for each choice and seeing how it fits with what we want or like or enjoy.

❖ Looking at how much effort each choice entails i.e. which is the easiest or the hardest.

❖ Thinking about how much change is involved for each choice.

❖ Thinking about how each choice fits in with our own beliefs or concepts.

❖ Thinking about how each choice fits in with our peers beliefs or concepts or wishes.

❖ Thinking about how each choice fits in with society's idea of 'normal'.

❖ Looking at how much each choice costs (not just financially but in any other way too).

❖ Thinking about how each choice affects other people.

❖ Thinking about how each choice affects us in the short-term i.e. the 'now'.

❖ Thinking about how each choice affects us in the long-tem i.e. the 'future'.

❖ Does it feel 'right'?

❖ And lastly, simply acting without any thought of the consequences or even any thought as to why we even made the choice.

There are very likely more thought processes that we can go through before we reach a decision, but everyone probably goes through at least one of the above when faced with a decision.

To start following our intuition, we firstly have to connect to our higher self, our intuitive voice. We need to hear our intuitive voice before we can listen to it. That voice needs to be loud and it needs to be clear. As we have said earlier, for that to happen, we need to connect to our higher self and then we need to nurture and develop that connection. There are many ways of learning to connect to our intuition, through meditation, through physical practices like Yoga, through prayer, through stillness and silence, through focused intention and so on. In Reiki terms we achieve this by self-healing and through 'right thinking and right living'. By doing this we can become more intuitive with our healing work as well as our path.

Trusting our intuition will allow us to make choices that are more in line with our true path. As we start to follow our higher path we get closer to the Divine and to our higher self and we move away from our physical self. The voice of our lowest base nature becomes quieter as our higher self becomes louder. Eventually the only voice we hear is that of our higher self, our intuition. When we are faced with choices and decisions to make, we make them from a place of awareness, from a place of understanding. We no longer make choices for physical desires or personal pleasure or gain, but for our higher spiritual good.

At this time we are guided by our intuition, all our choices are the right choices for us as individuals and for everyone whose life we touch, however distantly it may appear. This is a fundamental shift in the way we live our lives, but it is a vital one for our spiritual growth.

Chapter Twenty

The Core of Reiki

The Three Energy Bodies

Usui-sensei saw human beings as being composed of three distinct interconnected bodies: the physical body, the emotional body and the spiritual body. In every human being there is a physical centre (just below the navel,) an emotional centre (the heart area) and a spiritual centre (the third eye – mid forehead). Usui-sensei discovered and developed a method for healing all three bodies using specific energies that are accessed using the shirushi (symbols), jumon (name) and kotodama (mantra).

For complete healing and to obtain enlightenment, all three bodies need to be healed and united to become one. When you are born these three bodies are all connected in a state of oneness. As you live your life these bodies can drift apart, to a lesser or greater degree, because of your upbringing, social and peer pressures and the way you live your life. This can lead to inner conflict and loss of direction. You can be pulled in different directions if your emotions are sending you down one path, your spiritual nature is barely heard and your physical body pursues physical pleasures and material success.

This state of living can never result in true happiness or fulfilment and any happiness will be fleeting and superficial. To be truly happy you need to be in a state of oneness internally and externally (i.e. with yourself and with God or the Universe) where your intuition guides you and your thoughts and actions follow, without conflict or argument. This is the ultimate state for mankind to achieve and should be the goal of each and every individual.

When you are attuned to Reiki, regardless of where you are on your spiritual path or your physical life, it re-connects the three bodies. As you self-heal daily, the connection between your three bodies grows stronger and your intuition becomes louder and harder to ignore. The more you self-heal the closer you get to your true spiritual nature and you then become guided by your spiritual self. In time your emotional and physical bodies will be lead solely by your spiritual guidance and intuition and there will be no more inner conflict, as you journey on your higher path.

The Five Stages To Complete Your Spiritual Circle of Life

There are five stages to Usui Reiki Ryoho that culminate in enlightenment. You will go through all five stages throughout your life. There is no timescale for each stage, you will spend as long as you need at each stage.

Rei To Heal The Soul

By healing with high frequency Rei energy you can heal your soul and re-connect to your higher self. This helps you to remember who you are and why you are here i.e. discover your purpose and follow your higher path

CKR To Heal The Physical Body

Healing with the lower frequencies of the CKR allows you to heal any physical conditions that you may have. This will be an ongoing process as we all pick up physical traumas throughout our life.

SHK To Heal The Emotional Body

Healing with the higher frequencies of the SHK allows you to heal any mental/emotional conditions that you may have. This will be an ongoing process as we all pick up emotional traumas throughout our life.

HSZSN To Create Oneness

Using the HSZSN to connect to yourself allows you to use the CKR and SHK to heal past and future traumas. This will give balance and completeness within. You will find that oneness is experienced i.e. your mind, body and soul will be healed, connected, balanced and working as one.

DKM To Connect To God (or the Universe)

The DKM can only be truly understood once you are healed sufficiently. At this point you will be at your highest frequency. You will have the strongest possible connection to God (or the Universe) and will feel close to and part of God (or the Universe). You will be healed on all levels and will be living your life in the right way (for you). You will have all the answers you need, you will be content and at peace – life will make complete sense. This is enlightenment.

Rei to heal the soul

By healing with the high frequency Rei energy at this point you will be preparing yourself to move away from your physical life on Earth to your spiritual life with God (or the Universe).

It is worth remembering that Usui-sensei developed his Reiki Ryoho primarily as a spiritual path for self-development and enlightenment. As part of this process, healing the body and mind and soul are all necessary steps that need to be taken. It is a wonderful journey that will heal you on every level. It is up to you how far along this path you travel, your progress is limited only by you. The more you self-heal, the more you live your life in the right way for you, the further you will travel on your higher path, until ultimately you will attain the happiness that comes with enlightenment.

SECTION FOUR
REIKI THE HEALING ART

Chapter Twenty One

Choosing a Reiki Practitioner or Teacher

There are a range of different styles of Reiki and millions of Reiki practitioners worldwide, so it is no mean feat finding a professional and competent Reiki practitioner or teacher. It is essential to understand that there are many healers worldwide, who claim to be practicing Reiki, but for quite a number, their teachings are considerably different from what the founder, Usui-sensei meant by Reiki.

Reiki healers are responsible for giving their clients the most effective treatment they possibly can, with due regard for the client's medical condition and always taking into account the implications of medications the client has been prescribed. If there are any contraindications to the Reiki treatment, the practitioner should act appropriately and if necessary, refuse to treat the client, for the client's own protection and well-being.

A proficient Reiki practitioner should have a very solid underpinning knowledge of their subject and always put the client's welfare above their own personal interests. There are numerous practitioners who are driven by ego, as there are in other fields, so make sure you are completely comfortable with a practitioner or teacher prior to booking any treatments or courses.

Before you make the decision to go for a treatment or book a course we would advise you to give the practitioner or teacher a call first and ask them questions about how they use Reiki, what Reiki is, what the benefits are, and so on. If the response they give seems too vague or ambiguous, then you would be better off searching elsewhere.

Above and beyond all else, have faith in your own intuition. If something just does not feel right to you, then go with that feeling. Don't force yourself into a decision that makes you feel uncomfortable and don't let anyone else force you into such as decision. People often assume that because someone has spent years practicing Reiki, or because they are well-read on the subject, that they are a fantastic healer. In real terms these things are pretty meaningless. Being a good Reiki practitioner or teacher comes down to how much self-healing the individual does, their true understanding of Reiki and how they live their life.

Below you will find some criteria to look out for when deciding where to go for Reiki.

❑ Make sure the Reiki practitioner or teacher belongs to a relevant, recognised Reiki body. Regulations for Reiki differ depending on your country of residence. If your country has a register of suitably qualified practitioners and teachers, refer to this.

❑ Speak to the Reiki practitioner or teacher on the telephone prior to booking a session or course, to ensure that you are completely comfortable with their approach to Reiki. Listen carefully to what they say and make sure that they answer your questions appropriately and honestly.

Prepare a list of questions to ask the practitioner or teacher to gauge how they work with the energy and to ensure that their mode of practice suits you. Be aware that some teachers and practitioners do not work on conditions directly; they merely offer Reiki for relaxation.

So, if you have anything that requires treatment or if you want to learn Reiki in a way that will enable you to use it directly on specific conditions, you will need to go to a practitioner or teacher who works actively with the Reiki energy and will treat you accordingly. Active Reiki healers usually complete comprehensive interview forms with you and ensure that you are aware of the contraindications of Reiki, as well as treating your conditions directly.

❑ If you are planning on going for a Reiki treatment and you are female, we would advise that you either go and visit a female practitioner or take a friend with you for the initial treatment, for your own safety and peace of mind.

❑ Some Reiki teachers and practitioners offer distant attunements or treatments. It is essential if you want to learn how to use Reiki effectively and understand the system, to learn from a qualified teacher. Qualifications you receive for taking a distance course may not be recognised in some countries, or by some Reiki associations and insurers and if you pay for a distant treatment you will not know what sort of treatment you are getting, if any. For your own well-being it would be better for you to see a practitioner directly or if you are learning to attend a recognised Reiki course, where the teacher offers post-course support. Distant attunements can be completely ineffectual, especially if you are not taught any knowledge about Reiki.

❑ If you are intending to attend a Reiki course, make sure that the course is certified and that manuals and post-course support are provided. Some teachers do not provide manuals and this will make it incredibly difficult for you to practice Reiki proficiently after your course.

❑ Beware of Reiki teachers who loftily refer to themselves as Sensei's, Great Grand Master's or other such titles. Sensei is a term used by students for their teacher as a sign of respect. A teacher should not adopt the term as their title. The title of Great Grand Master is not relevant to traditional Usui Reiki. Usui-sensei believed that the teaching of Reiki should be straightforward and that teachers should be humble. Also be aware that Reiki is a very serious system of healing. If all a teacher is concerned with, is impressing you with their ability to perform party tricks using Reiki energy, then you would do best to steer clear. Reiki is not for improving the taste of wine, helping to find a car parking space or changing traffic lights, it is for healing purposes!

❑ The energy used in Reiki derives from one source, God or the Universe and uses all available healing frequencies. If a healing system that uses the term Reiki talks of connecting you to other energies, such as: the moon, stars, trees, planets, then it is not Usui Reiki Ryoho being taught.

❑ Some Reiki teachers offer cheap deals, allowing you to learn three Reiki levels in one weekend. It is not possible to become a good Reiki teacher in one weekend, or learn all the information necessary to teach effectively. Teaching Reiki is a big responsibility, as is providing healing. Taking all the levels in one weekend will leave you feeling disempowered, confused and deficient in the underlying knowledge of the system.

Attunements are integral to a Reiki course. If you are not attuned properly, you will not be able to heal effectively. A professional Usui Reiki Ryoho course should offer 4 attunements on level 1, 1 attunement on level 2 and 1 attunement on the master level. These numbers correspond to the number of attunements Usui-sensei gave to his students.

❑ Some Reiki teachers believe that attunements are not really necessary, or, that it is irrelevant how many attunements are given on a course. They claim that the teacher's intentions are enough to enable the student to use Reiki. Intention is never enough. Good intentions always have to be backed up by good actions, in any area of life, or those intentions will never amount to anything.

The attunement process connects you to the source of the energy. Attunements are an integral part of any Reiki course. We have had to re-attune a number of students that have attended our courses because after taking courses with other teachers, they have become disillusioned with Reiki and are not able to heal effectively, as a result of not being attuned correctly.

❑ Usui Reiki Ryoho attunements do not utilise singing bowls, Tibetan bells, gongs, or any other paraphernalia that bears no relation to traditional Usui Reiki attunements. If any of the aforementioned are utilised as part of the attunement process, you are not receiving a Usui Reiki Ryoho attunement. Prior to attending a course it might be a good idea to ask the teacher some information about the attunements they offer.

❑ Some Reiki teachers offer Reiju or empowerments instead of attunements. Depending on the version of Reiju being used, you may need to receive Reiju on an on-going basis until you reach the level of connection required for the course you are taking. This will need to be explained to you by the teacher and arrangements made for you to receive Reiju either in-person or distantly. Usui-sensei used an early form of Reiju on students he saw regularly to raise their vibrational frequency in small incre-ments, enabling the student, after a great deal of practice, to eventually use Reiki for healing. Along with the Reiju, Usui-sensei would expect his students to undertake a variety of meditations to raise their frequency, such as Hatsu Rei Ho. He gave later forms of Reiju or attunements to the students he saw only on short course, to raise their frequency much more rapidly, without the need for other meditation based techniques. By doing this students were able to heal immedi-ately (after been taught the correct method for connecting to the energy and healing). If in doubt, always ask the teacher what they mean by 'Reiju' and 'attunements' and make sure you are happy they know and understand what they are doing.

❑ There is no gap required between level 1 and 2. If a teacher suggests to you that there needs to be a gap between these levels, you would be better off looking elsewhere. It is preferable to learn these two courses together, as intended by the founder of Reiki, Usui-sensei. Level 1 Reiki is a stepping stone to level 2 and enables you to heal only on a spiritual level. We all have emotional and physical traumas that require healing and it is only once you have taken your level 2 course that you are able to heal on these levels.

The attunements on the courses instigate a cleansing process within you and if you have only learned level 1 Reiki you will not be able to effectively heal yourself through the cleansing process. Students who learn level 1 without level 2 can often become disenchanted with Reiki because they are only able to offer a high frequency healing that does not work directly on physical and emotional conditions. This can lead to such students abandoning Reiki because they do not feel that it is an effective mode of healing. Level 1 offers only Rei healing and level 2 provides the full Reiki healing. Along with Usui-sensei, Dr Chujiro Hayashi also taught these courses together, over five days, for two hours on each day.

❑ Ensure that any practitioner or teacher you are planning on visiting for a treatment or course has a lineage, which extends back to the founder of Reiki, Usui-sensei.

❑ It's a good idea to ask a Reiki practitioner if they recommend ongoing treatments or if they only provide treatments for a set period of time. A professional and ethical Reiki practitioner should not see a client for more than 5-10 treatments (unless the client has a serious or terminal condition that requires ongoing treatment). We find that we don't usually need to see clients for more than 5 treatments and we aim to improve their condition in as short a time as possible. Some Reiki healers will happily treat an individual for years on end but this is not a good way to empower the client. The aim should be to get the client back to good health rapidly, enabling them to take responsibility for their personal well-being.

❑ Avoid Reiki practitioners or teachers who have mammoth egos. Reiki is a precious gift from God or the Universe and is infinite and limitless in its potential. A good Reiki practitioner will be highly responsible in their approach, be humble in the face of Reiki and treat whatever their client comes to them for.

❑ Reiki has contraindications and a professional and competent Reiki practitioner or teacher should be willing to address these contraindications with their clients or students. There are certain circumstances when it is unsafe for the client to be given a Reiki treatment. A good Reiki practitioner or teacher should never put their client's or student's health at risk. If a Reiki practitioner or teacher claims that, "Reiki can do no harm" or that "intention is all that matters," they are avoiding taking responsibility in their role.

❑ Be discerning with any information that is presented to you, whether in the form of a book or conversation. Trust in your intuition. A Reiki practitioner or teacher well-read on the subject does not automatically make them proficient at Reiki.

❑ Before you go for a treatment or course ask the practitioner or teacher if they self-heal regularly. If they never self-heal look elsewhere.

Chapter Twenty Two

What to Expect from a Reiki Treatment

A Reiki treatment should be tailored to each individual, should look at physical and emotional conditions and symptoms, as well as explore lifestyle issues that may be contributing to ill health. A good Reiki practitioner should aim to work directly on the conditions and symptoms presented to them by the client and should encourage the client to take responsibility for their own life. This way the client can leave with a greater sense of empowerment and knowledge that they have received the best treatment possible from that practitioner.

To begin the treatment a Reiki practitioner should have a chat with their client about Reiki, give a brief summary of what Reiki is, as many people will know very little about the therapy and answer any questions the client may have about Reiki in general or the treatment they are about to undergo. Having a general comprehension of Reiki and the experience they are about to go through will put the client at ease and foster their confidence in the practitioner's abilities.

The practitioner should then complete an interview form with their client to establish what conditions they are suffering from if any, and what specifically needs treatment. At the very minimum, the practitioner should at least take the client's name, address, date of birth, telephone number, doctor's address, doctor's diagnosis and any medication that has been prescribed.

A good Reiki practitioner should then ask the client other questions about all their symptoms, physical, emotional and spiritual, their life stresses which may have contributed to or directly caused their condition, their lifestyle, sleeping habits and other appropriate questions.

From this the practitioner can assess what kind of treatment is needed and aim to treat the conditions the client is presenting them with. This procedure instigates the healing process, as the client is able to express their feelings before a non-judgmental listener and to consciously externalise feelings that they may have kept suppressed previously, perhaps even for a lifetime. Additionally the client learns the value of their intuition by voicing the choices they already know they need to make in life.

The client should then read through the interview form to make sure all the information is accurate and sign to say they agree with what has been written and to give consent for the treatment.

Following this most necessary procedure, the Reiki treatment should take place. The client lays fully clothed on a treatment couch with their eyes closed. The practitioner will then place their hands in various positions above the client's body channelling energy at the correct frequency to work on the presenting conditions of the client. The treatment can last between 45 minutes and 2 hours depending on each individual client and their needs.

The practitioner is not restricted by a set series of hand positions but works differently according to individual needs. If the client presents the practitioner with a specific illness or injury, such as a broken bone, the practitioner should work directly on the damaged bone to offer the best possible treatment. Any other underlying issues that may need attention can be addressed in subsequent treatments, after the primary condition has been tended to.

Following the treatment, the practitioner should discuss the client's experiences and anything else the client would like to talk about. The client should be allowed the time to rest for as long as they need to and to have the time to discuss anything that arose from their treatment, without feeling they are being rushed out of the door.

People's experiences of Reiki are very individual and depend on where the client is physically, emotionally and spiritually. Some people will only wish to have a Reiki session for relaxation and will find themselves feeling much calmer and more serene after their treatment. For other people, Reiki is a life-changing event. If the client has a condition they should expect improvements in the state of their condition with every treatment, whether that condition is physical, emotional or spiritual.

It is not essential, but recommended that a treatment form is completed for each session with the client to quantify improvements in their physical and emotional conditions and symptoms. This allows both the practitioner and the client to see how the conditions and symptoms are responding to each treatment. In addition the forms can serve as data for scientific research into Reiki.

How Many Treatments Do I Need?

There is no set number of Reiki treatments a client will need, it is dependent on each individual, their presenting conditions, their circumstances, lifestyle and emotional traumas.

Everyone responds to the stresses and events life presents them with in different ways and there is no magic instant cure all formula. In saying that though, you shouldn't have to be going to see a Reiki practitioner for years on end. We have found with our practice of Reiki that generally a client will need between 1 and 12 treatments, depending on the severity of their conditions. Most people will be empowered enough to make healthy choices and their condition will have made enormous progress after about 4 or 5 treatments. For those with mental illnesses, cancer and other terminal conditions the client must be treated for the duration of their illness. We cannot emphasise enough that if someone comes to a Reiki practitioner with cancer the practitioner must make it clear to the client that they will require treatment for the duration of their condition. We feel it is unethical to charge a fee to clients with cancer. In these circumstances we would teach the client and their family a basic Reiki course, enabling them to treat themselves on a daily basis for the rest of their life. This way the client and their family gain a sense of control over the condition.

Chapter Twenty Three

Contraindications to Reiki

As with many other complementary therapies, there are contraindications to Reiki, or more accurately, there are certain medical conditions that need to be treated with caution, contrary to the beliefs of many Reiki practitioners and teachers worldwide.

To be a responsible, ethical and competent Reiki practitioner or teacher it is essential to inform your students or clients about the possible effects Reiki may have with regards to certain medical conditions and the medications involved.

We have heard Reiki teachers say that if the condition improves the Reiki energy is so intelligent it will stop the medication harming the client, or others have said the Reiki energy will force the excess medication out of the body and leave just the right level. This is so far-fetched as to be ridiculous. It is avoiding responsibility to say that the Reiki energy will always *know* what to treat, as many Reiki healers around the world do. The energy does not *know* what medication and what dosage a client is on and will not adjust the medication accordingly, all by itself as their condition improves and a lower dosage is required. This idea is ludicrous and potentially harmful to clients.

The first thing to consider when thinking about the contraindications with regards to Reiki is do you believe Reiki can treat an illness or injury and cause an improvement in the condition? The evidence we have seen both with our own healing work and that of our students has demonstrated the efficacy of Usui Reiki Ryoho when used in an active way.

If you believe that Reiki can cause improvement to a condition, clinical or otherwise, then it follows that if a client is taking prescribed medication for that condition, the medication may need to be reduced, depending on the condition and the medication. Think about something like an under-active thyroid gland for which something like Thyroxine is prescribed. The dosage prescribed is adjusted to suit each individual and their specific level of thyroid function. If the level of thyroid function changes, as in the case of a Reiki client whose condition improves after one or more treatments, surely it is simple common sense that the dosage of Thyroxine will need to be adjusted to compensate for any changes?

There are certain conditions whereby when or if the Reiki will heal, or at the very least improve that condition the very improvement can cause a potential overdose in the prescribed medication the client is taking.

When deciding on whether a client's condition and medication may need to be monitored by their doctor you need to have a clear understanding of the condition and the effects of the medication. It is best to ask the client about their medication and what it actually does for them. You should also research the client's condition and medication to get a deeper understanding if you need to. You can then decide if the medication may become harmful if the condition changes and improves. If you feel it will become harmful then it is your responsibility as a practitioner to inform your client and advise them to contact their doctor before you give them any treatments. Their doctor needs to monitor their condition and adjust the dosage of medication as the condition improves. If their doctor is unwilling to do this, then the safest course of action for a good practitioner would be to refuse to treat the client in these circumstances, as they can be held responsible if the client experiences any adverse reactions. Furthermore a good Reiki practitioner should not be risking their client's health.

Chapter Twenty Four

The Hand Positions

The well-known Western hand positions, were developed by Mrs Takata, possibly with some help from Dr Hayashi. These hand positions offer a simple way for Reiki practitioners to give treatments at the beginning of their Reiki journey. They were developed to allow students with little or no intuitive ability and those with little or no sensitivity to the energy to give reasonably effective treatments. These hand positions are:

The Head Area

  Front of face
  Sides of head
  Back of head
  Front of neck/throat

The Front Of The Body

  Just above the chest
  Just below the chest
  By the navel
  Just below the stomach (groin area)

Back

  Shoulders
  High up on rib cage
  Lower back

Base of spine

Arms

Shoulders
Elbows
Wrists
Hands

Legs

Hips
Knees
Ankles
Feet

Generally the hand positions used are the Head Area, Front Of The Body and the Back. These hand positions allow for a general all-over treatment by putting energy into the main energy meridians, the brain area, the throat area, the internal organs and the body's main systems. The hand positions for the arms and legs are generally only used if there are specific problems in those areas, although some practitioners use all the hand positions. These are still taught by many Reiki teachers, and for some Reiki teachers these are the only hand positions that can be used for any treatment.

Although this is a very simple method to use, it does limit the effectiveness of the treatment. As the practitioner keeps their hands in any one position for a few minutes, only a small amount of energy is used for each position. This may be fine for people with no illness or injury, but for someone with a medical condition, a few minutes of treatment is no where near enough to give effective healing. These hand positions by their simple nature are incredibly easy to learn and just as easy to teach. Perhaps our culture of wanting everything now and without too much effort was a factor in Mrs Takata's thinking. This is perhaps why Mrs Takata used them when she taught Reiki in the West.

In the Usui Reiki Ryoho Hikkei there are details of specific hand positions to treat many illnesses and injuries. Usui-sensei taught practitioners to treat any condition directly by placing their hands over the problem area. He is quoted as saying *"If brain disease occurs, I treat a head. If it's a stomachache, I treat a stomach. If it's an eye disease, I treat eyes"* At the early stages of their training, practitioners would use the hand positions from the handbook, but as they developed their understanding and intuitive ability they would use Byosen Reikan Ho (A form of scanning using the hands) and/or their intuition to locate the areas that needed treatment.

In this way the practitioner gives treatment on the area that needs it for the duration of the treatment maximising the benefit to the client. This is by far the most effective way to treat specific conditions.

Chapter Twenty Five

How to Work with Reiki Effectively

There are many ways in which Reiki is taught and practiced. Again, there are many differences of opinion between Reiki teachers about the best way to give effective treatments. Some Reiki teachers believe that because Reiki is an individual journey, practitioners can carry out treatments in the way that they have been taught or the way they want to and it makes no difference what they do or how they do it. For many Reiki practitioners and teachers Reiki is nothing more than a means of relaxation.

This is not actually the case. The way Reiki is practiced makes a difference to the effectiveness of the treatment. The more effective the treatment is, the more the client will benefit.

The process is very simple and can be broken down into three steps:

Step 1

Determine what you are going to treat

Step 2

Connect to the energy

Step 3

Treat the relevant areas

Of course how this is done is incredibly important and the details are as follows:

Step 1: Determine What You Are Going To Treat

There are a number of ways to determine what to treat for each client. One way is to use Byosen Reikan Ho, which is an effective way of locating specific areas that need treatment. Once the areas are identified, suitable treatment can be given. Although you can identify areas that need treatment with Byosen Reikan Ho, you cannot always determine whether each area requires physical or emotional healing by this method, so use a combination of your intuitive feeling and discussion with the client. Using Byosen Reikan Ho requires confidence in yourself and your ability. The only way to become proficient and therefore confidant is to practice as much as you can, and in any case, as much as you need to.

Another way is to simply ask the client if they have any physical or emotional conditions that they would like treatment for.

The most effective way is to complete an interview form or a record form for the client to determine what needs treating and if they have any medical conditions that need treating or that could contraindicate with Reiki. You can use Byosen Reikan Ho as well to locate where to treat the client if it is not apparent from the form. This process can be as involved and thorough as you make it. Basically, the more information you have, the more effectively you can treat the client.

The first thing you need to know once you have taken down their name/address/contact details is their medical condition and any prescribed medication they are taking.

Make a note of all their diagnosed medical conditions. If you are not sure what the medical terms mean, ask the client or research the information yourself before the next treatment. Ensure that there are absolutely no contraindications with the medication/conditions before you treat the client. If the client does not have any medical conditions, ask them about the symptoms they are experiencing that indicate to them they are not in good physical or emotional health.

The next thing you should be looking at is what other symptoms the client is experiencing at the moment. Try to get the client to look at themselves in a detached and objective way. Make a note of all of these additional symptoms as well. It is a good idea at this stage to ask the client to look at their condition and their symptoms and see if there is an underlying reason for the way they feel. This is a good way to empower the client to take responsibility for their well-being.

The next stage is to look for any emotional traumas that may be causing or aggravating their conditions. Ask the client to look back at their life and see what events have caused them emotional upset. The events do not necessarily have to be major ones, even small events can cause emotional pain. These emotional traumas can, if left untreated, eventually have a direct adverse physical effect on the body.

To give the most effective course of treatments you need to work on the physical and/or emotional symptoms and any underlying emotional traumas associated with them. It is better to treat one condition at a time, this way you can channel the energy effectively, to meet the requirements of each condition. In any case, you should not use more than one healing shirushi (symbol) at a time. For the most part, it is much more effective to treat the symptom first, especially if the symptom is causing damage to the body. On other occasions it can be more effective to treat the emotional trauma that is directly responsible for the symptom first. It all depends on the individual client and their conditions and situation.

We cannot give you a fixed rule to follow. You have to assess each individual case on its merits. Generally though, we tend to treat any physical damage to the body first and then the emotional causes afterwards. Where there is no physical damage, only pain, we treat the emotional causes first.

One final thing, it is always advisable to refer your clients to a medical professional for a diagnosis if they have come to you for treatment, unless of course they have come purely for a relaxation treatment.

Once you have decided what you are going to treat, use the relevant energy. Connect to the energy using the relevant shirushi and its jumon (name) and kotodama (mantra).

Step 2: Connect To The Energy

See chapter 13 'The Reiki Energies' section 'How To Use The Shirushi And Their jumon And Kotodama' for full details.

Step 3: Treat The Relevant Area(s)

Put your hands in position to start the treatment. Ensure you are channelling energy externally, through the relevant shirushi. Use intention and visualisation to maximise the healing effects of the energy. Stay as focused as you can when giving Reiki treatments – the more focused you are the more focused the energy becomes. If your mind drifts away bring it back with kotodama and/or intention and/or visualisation.

Keep your hands in position for as long as you need to. If the client has an injury or illness in one place, spend all the treatment time at that position to maximise the healing effects. If you are working on more than one area, you should apportion the treatment time in each area to give the most effective healing. You can do this by intuition and sensing the energy or by working on the conditions with regards to their severity and harm to the client. Obviously the more harmful and severe the condition is, the more time and energy you need to give it.

Chapter Twenty Six

The Clinical Nature of Reiki

One aspect of Reiki that seems to have been lost over the years is the clinical application of Reiki. In Usui-sensei's era, Reiki was a well-respected therapy used to treat many illnesses and injuries. We know, for example, that Usui-sensei and Dr Hayashi both treated clinical conditions, and Dr Hayashi had his own clinic. Mrs Takata herself describes the treatments she was given at Dr Hayashi's clinic for her many illnesses. We know from our own practice how effective Reiki is in treating medical conditions.

We teach Reiki as a clinical practice and have always done so. Many of our students go on to work on clinical conditions themselves and the feedback we get from them is very positive. Reiki is an effective therapy that can be used to treat people safely and professionally in a clinical environment. as long as it is practiced in the correct manner.

So how do Reiki practitioners fit into a clinical environment? The first thing to ensure is good training and practice. If you want to work in a clinical environment, such as a hospice or hospital, you need to make sure you are trained to work in a safe and professional way. You need to have an awareness of, and follow the hygiene requirements for the establishment.

Reiki now seems to be relegated to the realms of 'relaxation therapies' used to help people to relax primarily and to deal with the stresses and pains of their medical conditions, whether they are the symptoms of an illness or the aftermath of an operation. It is hard to know when or why this change occurred. It is conceivable that because Reiki in the West was spread by such a small group of teachers initially (the 22 masters of Takata) that any changes instigated by any of them would have been taught to many students. Some of these students became teachers and passed on the changes to many more students...and so on, until what started as an incorrect interpretation or mistake, or even a deliberate change, became accepted as fact, simply because it was taught to so many people. Perhaps in this way the clinical nature of Reiki was lost over the years.

It is also possible that because teaching Reiki as a relaxation therapy rather than a clinical therapy is easier for both the teacher and the students, this became the accepted norm that suited both parties. For whatever reason or combination of reasons Reiki teaching and practice has changed over the years.

Working In A Clinical Environment

Working as a therapist in a hospital or hospice can be incredibly rewarding and fulfilling. The first step is to contact the institution where you would like to offer Reiki. Many hospitals and hospices have a volunteer department that manages and provides a wide range of voluntary services, one of which may be a volunteer therapist service. Some have paid therapists as well, so do your research before you call, to make sure you get through to the right department.

It is important to be prepared before you make the telephone call. You may be asked a variety of questions about yourself and about Reiki, so you will need to have ready answers. Expect to be asked what Reiki is, how Reiki works, what the benefits of Reiki are, how Reiki would fit into their environment, how much experience you have as well as many other questions.

You need to sound professional and knowledgeable, so prepare beforehand. You may be asked to give a sample treatment to determine both your ability and your suitability.

If, as a Reiki practitioner or teacher, you want to work in a hospice or hospital, either as a volunteer therapist or even a paid therapist, there are certain standards and guidelines you will need to adhere to. One vital question to ask is whether you will be treating patients for their conditions to improve them (i.e. to give a healing treatment) or whether you will be treating patients to relieve symptoms of stress and anxiety and possibly reduce pain. This will dictate the way you work with the Reiki energy. Obviously every hospital and hospice will have their own guidelines, so here we have included some as an example of the kind of things to expect:

❑ Therapists must have the required qualifications. For Reiki generally this is a level 2 certificate.

❑ Therapists must have professional therapy insurance for Reiki practice.

❑ Therapists must observe the hygiene and cleanliness rules for the particular hospital or hospice. This is of the utmost importance - remember hospitals and hospices are essentially sterile environments to protect both the patients and the staff.

❑ If there is a dress code, follow it. This includes the wearing of jewellery and watches on the hands and lower arms.

❑ Therapists will be expected to adhere to any Health and Safety, Diversity, Equal Opportunities, Sex Discrimination and Race Discrimination policies as well any other relevant policies that apply.

❑ Therapists must respect the confidentiality of the patients and may be asked to complete and sign a patient confidentiality form.

❏ Therapists may only treat patients with their explicit approval.

❏ Treatment records should be kept and updated for each treatment. These forms are normally provided by the hospital or hospice.

❏ Therapists must inform a relevant staff member if they notice any changes to or have any concerns about a patient's health or well-being.

❏ Therapists are not generally allowed to offer their services as private practitioners. This is not an opportunity to get more clients.

❏ Therapists need to be aware of any contraindications for Reiki and work accordingly.

❏ Therapists must respect the right of patients to refuse their offer of treatment.

❏ Therapists must make themselves aware of the patient's conditions through the use of patient notes and if necessary by asking a relevant member of staff and work accordingly.

Hopefully this will give you a rough idea of what to expect when working in a hospital or hospice. You should always refer to the establishment itself for a complete set of guidelines.

SECTION FIVE

THE REIKI PATH

Chapter Twenty Seven

Reiki Courses

Can Anyone Learn Reiki?

Potentially anyone that wants to learn Reiki can learn Reiki. Any qualified Reiki master/teacher can connect a student to the source of the energy and teach them how to use the energy for healing themselves and others. There are no pre-requisites or specialist knowledge needed to take a Reiki course. There is no need for any religious or spiritual belief system. Reiki is not a religion, nor is it a spiritual doctrine, though Reiki can be a spiritual path. Reiki is simple, natural and easy to learn and Usui-sensei believed that the teaching of Reiki should be, in his own words "easy and common as possible, nothing lofty."

However, in saying that anyone can learn Reiki, not everyone will choose to do this and not everyone that learns Reiki will practice and develop it.

What To Expect From A Reiki Course

Reiki courses differ enormously depending on what teacher you go to. Remember that there are over 140 different types of Reiki and so many people have added their own hallmark onto Reiki to make them seem more original, innovative and perhaps ultimately to make more money. Just to give you an idea, a few of the many types of Reiki include: Alchemia Reiki, Gold Reiki, Imara Reiki, Karuna Reiki, Kundalini Reiki, Seichem Reiki, Seichim Reiki, Sekhem Reiki, Tera Mai Reiki, Tibetan Reiki, the list goes on and on.

We cannot give you any idea what to expect from the many different types of Reiki in existence today but we can tell you what you should expect from a Reiki course in the traditional style of Usui-sensei.

There should be either three or four levels that go from beginner to master/teacher. Traditionally Usui-sensei taught Reiki with seven main levels and sub-levels within these, due to his martial arts background, but he worked with Hayashi-sensei to develop Reiki into 1st, 2nd and 3rd level formats, with sub-levels within the three main levels. All courses should include a comprehensive manual, certificate and free post course support for all students. The cost of Reiki courses varies between different teachers and styles of Reiki. We suggest you see what the average cost is in your location for the course you want to do and find a teacher that charges roughly that kind of price. Many Reiki teachers will offer discounts to students wishing to take their courses if they cannot afford the full price.

Reiki Level 1 Shoden

Reiki Level 1 is really a beginner level, and is known as Shoden, and is primarily for self-development and self-healing with the high frequency Rei or spiritual energy. No prior knowledge of Reiki is needed to take this course. Level 1 teaches you basic Reiki techniques as well as a great deal of knowledge.

The Rei energy you will connect to and channel at this level is used to work on the spiritual body and does not enable you to heal directly on a physical or emotional level. Having said that, there will always be indirect healing across all three energy bodies as they are interconnected. A Reiki teacher should make this very clear to you when you inquire about a Reiki course.

After a level 1 course you will not generally be able to heal specific physical or emotional conditions directly, you will primarily be healing yourself on a spiritual level. Obviously healing your spiritual body will improve your emotional and physical well-being, through the Rei energy filtering through your spiritual body into your emotional body and then into your physical body. This process of energy filtering through the various energy bodies can take some time, maybe months or even years.

Level 1 Reiki also begins the process of enlightenment, if taught correctly, raising your awareness and re-connecting you to the source of the energy or God or the Universe.

Some students after level 1 experience a sense of frustration that they now have this healing gift but are unable to heal themselves as effectively as they would wish to. It should be made clear to the student that once they have taken level 2, they will be able to heal themselves and others much more effectively, targeting specific physical and emotional conditions.

There should be 4 attunements on a level 1 course. Contrary to what some Reiki practitioners espouse, it does matter how many attunements you have, the attunement process is an integral part of Reiki and if you are not attuned in the correct way you will not be able to heal yourself or others effectively.

Alternatively Reiju empowerments can be used instead of attunements on the course, but Reiju empowerments may need to be given on a regular basis after the course until the student has reached the required level of energy connection and healing ability through the regular practice of Hatsu Rei Ho and self-healing.

A level 1 course should last one day or two at the most and no shirushi (symbols) should be included, these should be taught at level 2. There are variations to this, some courses teach the use of the CKR at level 1, and colleges tend to teach Reiki over a number of weeks, with one or two hours teaching each week.

Below you can find the syllabus we teach for a level 1 course. Parts of the syllabus are, we feel, essential when teaching Reiki, others are important but not necessarily essential. Look out for these elements when you search for a Reiki teacher to make sure you are getting the most professional and high quality course available.

Meaning Of The Word Reiki

It is important to understand what Reiki is and how it works. The deeper a student's grasp of Reiki, the more confidence they will have in the system itself, and in themselves as Reiki practitioners. We teach the meaning of both the Reiki kanji and the system of Reiki in traditional and modern terms. We also teach about the scientific research that has been carried out into energy healing and the scientific theories that now go a long way in explaining the mechanism of energy healing.

Reiki Attunements And Reiju Empowerments

The attunement or empowerment process is essential to Reiki and should be explained to students. The effects of this process are life changing and the students need to fully comprehend this.

History Of Reiki

There are a variety of stories and theories relating to the history of Reiki and of Usui-sensei. It is important for students to know as much of the real and factual history of Reiki as possible. Understanding the history and origins of Reiki helps students to understand the techniques and methods of Reiki more deeply.

Reiki Lineage

A Reiki teacher's lineage is important because for Reiki to be Usui Reiki Ryoho the lineage needs to start with Usui-sensei. The line of teachers that follow between Usui-sensei and any teacher indicate the type of Reiki taught by them. Needless to say, the shorter the lineage back to Usui-sensei the better it should be, as there are less teachers to make changes to the original system.

Reiki Ideals Or Precepts (Gokai)

The Gokai are both essential and important to the system of Reiki. The Gokai should be taught and explained to students. The practice of meditating and reflecting with the Gokai should be explained. The Gokai represent Usui-sensei's ideal of 'right thinking and right living', which is a big part of any student's growth and development.

Seven Levels Of Reiki

This is something few Reiki teachers cover on their courses. It is interesting to compare the original seven level system with the more modern three level system. This helps to understand traditional Reiki on a deeper level, but is not essential to a Reiki course.

The Main Reiki Hand Positions

The teaching of the hand positions is essential to Reiki, as is teaching the students' how and when to use the standard hand positions. It is equally as important to teach when and how to work without using the standard hand positions.

Kanji Hand Positions

Kanji hand positions, similar in concept to mudras, are a useful part of Reiki. These come from the traditional Shinto belief system. Reiki can be practiced without the use of the kanji hand positions, but their use does enhance the system.

The Reiki Method For Healing

Teaching and practising the correct method for healing using the high frequency Rei spiritual energy is absolutely essential to every

Reiki course. Poor practice in connecting and channelling energy can lead to tiredness, fatigue and drain a practitioner's Ki or life-force energy.

Modern Method To Develop Focus

This is a method for developing the ability to channel energy effectively without the interference of the conscious part of the mind. This is a useful tool to help develop more focus when giving Reiki treatments, but not essential.

Rei Shower[2]

Rei shower is an aura cleansing technique introduced into Japanese Reiki after Usui-sensei, and as such is not a Usui Reiki technique. It is popular amongst some Reiki teachers and practitioners. It is neither essential nor important to a Reiki course.

Signs Of Release

These are indicators of the body releasing negative energy and are useful to know. Although not essential, they are important.

Grounding And Protection

There are a number of theories regarding the need to ground and protect when practising Reiki. This is not part of Usui Reiki Ryoho and is a more recent Western add-on. This is not essential or important to Reiki, but an awareness of grounding and protection can be useful.

Byosen Reikan Ho Or Scanning

An essential part of every Reiki course. Whether it is called by its

Japanese name of Byosen Reikan Ho or by its Western name of Scanning, this technique should be taught and practiced on the course.

Jakikiri Joka Ho

An essential part of every Reiki course. The correct use of Jakikiri Joka Ho should be taught.

Bio Feedback

Bio feedback refers to the sensations both the giver and receiver of Reiki energy may experience. Understanding why the sensations are felt and knowing what they mean is very useful. This is an important aspect of giving treatments that should be taught, but it is not essential.

The Law (with regards to practicing Reiki)

We feel this is essential to ensure every Reiki student works within the law. Obviously the law needs to be researched by the Reiki teacher as it applies to their country of practice.

Contraindications

This is absolutely essential for the safe practice of the students and any one that receives healing from them. The contraindications need to be explained fully and in detail.

Giving Reiki Treatments

We teach tips on how to give good, effective and safe treatments. This is not essential, but allows us to share some of our experience of healing with our students.

21 day Cleansing Process

This is an essential part of any Reiki course. The cleansing process can be difficult for some students and they need to understand what is happening throughout the process and how to best deal with any changes that may occur.

Practice Healing

Time should be spent practising self-healing with the method taught on the course. The importance of self-healing should be explained.

Reiki Level 2 Okuden

Reiki Level 2 is the Ki part of Reiki and teaches the student to connect to and channel the lower frequency Ki energies. This level is generally regarded as the practitioner level and enables you to heal yourself and others on a physical and emotional, as well as spiritual level. This level also enables you to set yourself up as a Reiki practitioner should you wish to.

You must have already completed the level 1 Reiki as an entry requirement for this course. After taking this course you should be able to effectively treat conditions directly and understand how to be a professional Reiki practitioner, along with the responsibilities this brings. Your level of awareness should continue to expand as you make further headway along your higher path.

There should be one attunement on this course and this attunement allows you to use the shirushi to heal specific physical and emotional conditions.

Alternatively Reiju empowerments can be used instead of attunements on the course, but Reiju empowerments may need to be given on a regular basis after the course until such time the student has reached the required level of healing ability.

Three shirushi should be given to you at level 2. We will not give their names here as these symbols are sacred and the names of these symbols should only be given to you at level 2. We will refer to them as CKR, SHK and HSZSN.

CKR is the shirushi for physical healing energy, allowing you to work on the physical body and SHK is shirushi for the emotional energy healing, allowing you to work on the emotional body. The geometry and colour of these shirushi dictates the frequency of the energy you use to heal with.

The HSZSN is the shirushi for 'oneness' and is made up of three kanji. This shirushi allows you to specify a path to send energy across, for example you can send SHK energy to treat emotional issues from past traumas, you can send CKR energy to treat physical trauma to anyone or anything.

There should be no other shirushi at this level of Reiki, unless you are learning a non-traditional type of Reiki where new symbols have been made up.

This course should last one day or two at the most, although colleges tend to teach the course over a longer period of time with one or two hours teaching each week.

It is preferable that Reiki level 1 and 2 be learned together, or closely one after the other allowing the student to more capably heal themselves through their cleansing process and through life in general, and, of course, to help the student heal others competently. You should also be given details of how to obtain practitioner insurance and membership of a Reiki association with this course.

Below you can find the syllabus we teach for a level 2 course:

Energy Frequency

This is a discussion of the different frequency of physical, emotional and spiritual healing energies. It includes an in-depth explanation of the relationship between the frequency of the Reiki energy channelled to the condition being treated to achieve effective healing. This relates back to the scientific theories of energy healing. This is important to the practice of Reiki as a clinical or healing therapy.

Reiki Lineage

As level 1

Reiki Ideals Or Precepts (Gokai)

As level 1

Avoiding 'Picking-Up' Energy From Clients

The effects of working as a healer for those that are 'magnetic' in nature and how to deal with them. This is important for those that tend to 'pick-up' pain and emotional distress from others.

The Reiki Symbols (Shirushi)

This is absolutely essential for every Reiki 2 course. The shirushi should be presented to the students. The correct use of each shirushi should be explained. The history behind the shirushi is important, but the correct use of the shirushi is essential, this includes correct and accurate drawing and visualisation of the shirushi, and how to use the relevant shirushi to treat any condition.

Kotodama And Jumon

The meaning of and correct use of kotodama and jumon is essential to the practice of Reiki. The correct use of kotodama and jumon, with the relevant shirushi should be taught.

Passive Reiki Healing And Active Reiki Healing

It is important to distinguish between 'passive' and 'active' Reiki healing. The difference in approach and practice should be discussed and explained fully. Active Reiki healing is more in line with Usui-sensei's teachings.

The Basic Foundation Reiki Methods

This is a description of the basic methods for Reiki treatments using all the relevant techniques from level 1 and level 2.

Gyoshi Ho

Healing through the breath method. This is a basic Reiki technique that needs to be taught.

Koki Ho

Healing through the eyes method. This is a basic Reiki technique that needs to be taught.

Hatsu Rei Ho

This is an important Reiki method, or rather a combination of techniques that make up one distinct method. There are a number of versions of Hatsu Rei Ho practiced today, but there are some common elements to all the main versions. This method is not strictly speaking essential to the practice of Reiki but it is essential to know, as it forms part of the original teachings of Usui-sensei.

Professionalism With Clients

This is essential knowledge for a Reiki level 2 course. At this level a student can work as a professional therapist. To ensure that students will work in a professional and safe way, sufficient information and knowledge needs to be taught.

The Interview And Treatment Forms

We teach students to keep written records for each client. We provide both interview and treatment forms for this purpose. This is not essential, but it is extremely important to ensure good practice.

Working As A Reiki Practitioner

Teaching students about how to set up as a professional therapist is important but not essential. It is helpful to teach students about tax issues, marketing and advertising, therapist insurance, joining a Reiki association and where to practice.

The Reiki Method Using Symbols

This is essential. Teaching students how to connect to the relevant energy using the shirushi, jumon and kotodama and use the energy to give effective treatments is fundamental to good Reiki practice.

Giving Reiki Treatments

This expands from the basic methods from level 1 and gives more detailed and effective ways of giving treatments.

Practice Reiki

Students should be supervised while they practice giving Reiki treatments. Usually these are self-healing, healing others and distant or remote healing. In addition some teachers practice 'beaming' a method of sending energy to someone within your sight.

Relaxation Methods

We teach some basic relaxation methods to enable students to give their clients a way of dealing with their stress and tension in their own environment.

Reiki Level 3 Shinpiden

Traditionally Usui-sensei taught a separate mastership and beginner teacher mastership and these would be split into levels 3 and 4. At level 3 students would traditionally learn the so called 'mystery teachings'. We do not have a great deal of information about these teachings, but we do know they included subjects such as spiritualism, mysticism, numerology, healing methods and psychic ability.

Students would normally specialise in one of these areas. However, much of the information relating to this level is not available. Some Reiki teachers have made a level 3 out of the limited information that is available with some modern add-ons to complete the syllabus. How closely these resemble the original teachings of Usui-sensei is open to question.

A beginner teacher traditionally at level 4, would be able to specialise in the area where their proficiency lies. We do not know in the West exactly what Usui-sensei taught for the level 3 healing mastership, although we have elements of his teachings. For this reason when you are searching for a course you will notice that different Reiki teachers may or may not offer a healing mastership. Some teachers offer Reiki level 1, 2 and 3 (with level 3 being a teaching mastership), some offer levels 1, 2, 3 (healing mastership with more Western techniques) and 4 (teaching mastership), others split the healing and teaching mastership elements into a level 3a and 3b.

It really does differ across the board. Be aware that if you undertake a healing mastership, you will be learning a number of Western techniques as well as traditional Japanese techniques because we do not have all of Usui-sensei's teachings from this level.

What we have done ourselves is to split the course into a level 3 healing mastership and a level 4 teaching mastership. On level 3 we teach a combination of Western and Japanese techniques. The course is aimed at professional therapists working primarily with clinically ill clients, who would like to enhance their healing abilities and techniques. It is not always essential or necessary to learn level 3, you can go straight to a teaching mastership but we recommend that for people who would like to treat a wide range of clients with different clinical conditions it is best to undertake the healing mastership, so that you will have at your disposal a variety of methods to treat physical and emotional conditions.

Not everyone will need to learn a healing mastership, because for some people their intuition is so strong that they already have awareness of how to deal with different conditions, but this is not the case for everyone.

The Japanese elements we teach for this course are Reiji- ho, Chiryo and the Ryoho Shishon (guide to method of healing) and the course lasts for two days.

Below you can find the syllabus that we teach for a Level 3 course:

Rainbow Reiki

This is a practical method to determine the most effective frequency of energy to treat any condition.

Intention And Visualisation

The importance of using both intention and visualisation is

discussed and suitable intentions and visualisations are given. Reference is made to the scientific study of energy healing with intention and visualisation.

CKR Vortex

This is a method of removing the energy and pain associated with past emotional trauma.

Breathing

The importance of good breathing is discussed and a number of breathing techniques are taught.

Stress

A number of breathing and relaxation exercises to help reduce the damaging effects of stress are provided.

Treating Emotional Traumas

This is a method for treating deep-rooted emotional traumas, both past and present.

Depression

This is a simple method to use with clients suffering from depression. Clients can use this technique for themselves, so it is in effect empowering the client.

Bereavement

This is a method for treating clients who are suffering from a bereavement or loss of some kind.

Cancer

Specific methods to use when working with clients with cancer are provided, including: Reiki treatments, intention, visualisation, affirmations, stress reduction methods and addressing lifestyle issues.

Allergies

This is a method to treat the immune system to help alleviate allergic responses.

Healing Addictions

This is a method to reduce the need for any addiction.

Occasional Headaches

This is a simple method using visualisation to remove the energy causing a headache.

Migraines

This is a method to reduce the pain of a migraine at the time of treatment and to reduce the occurrence of migraines in general.

Injured Bones

This is a simple technique for treating broken bones.

ME And Low Energy

This is a method to treat clients with low energy.

Treating Causes Of Physical Illnesses

The importance of treating any underlying emotional traumas, conditions and stress that may be causing or aggravating the physical illness is discussed.

Clients With More Than One Illness

Methods to effectively treat clients with multiple illnesses are provided.

Moving Pains

This is a method for treating three types of 'moving pains,' that is, pain that refers as you try to treat it.

Schizophrenia

A series of techniques that can be used when working with clients suffering from schizophrenia are provided.

Insomnia

This is a simple technique for clients with insomnia, including self-help techniques.

Goal Setting And Problem Solving

A combination of powerful self-help tools to empower and motivate clients are taught.

Golden Frame Therapy

This is a simple and effective technique to help improve self-belief and motivate positive change.

The Reiki Crystal Grid

This is a method for using quartz crystals to enhance the Reiki energy for distant healing purposes.

Gassho Meditation

This is a meditation used widely in traditional Reiki.

Reiji-ho

This is a method to determine how to treat a client.

Chiryo

This is treatment in the traditional intuitive way.

Ryoho Shishon (guide to method of healing)

This is the healing guide from the Usui Reiki Hikkei, which we discuss and explain.

Teaching Mastership

Level 4, Shihan-Kaku, is the teaching mastership. This level is also called level 3 in the Western systems of Reiki. This course qualifies the student as a Reiki master/teacher and allows them to teach Reiki up to level 4, should they wish to do so. Some students prefer to learn this course purely for their own self-development or to enhance their healing abilities.

Taking a level 4 course is a huge responsibility as it enables the now Reiki master/teacher to guide students on their own higher paths. A good teacher should emphasise to their level 4 students the importance of understanding that they have now been given the ability to guide others and must do this with the utmost sense of responsibility and proficiency.

A good Reiki teacher is universally aware, has a great understanding of Reiki and how to pass Reiki onto others. They should have humility and infinite respect for the energy they are using and the source of that energy. Your teacher should emphasise the importance of spreading Reiki in an ethical and accountable way.

There is one attunement on this course and one shirushi, which we will refer to here as DKM. This shirushi provides the student with a direct connection to the source of the energy or God or the Universe. This increases the student's awareness, takes them closer to enlightenment and allows them to heal in a more effective way.

As a Reiki Master you should be creating a bridge between Heaven and Earth, God and humanity, the physical and the spiritual, so that you are able to guide people onto their higher paths. You become the link between man and God and should listen always to your intuition. Many Reiki Masters do not understand the gravity of their responsibility.

A Reiki Master course should last at least 2 to 4 days. A great deal of the time should be spent ensuring that the student is effectively able to give attunements and teach Reiki.

It is important to remember when you are teaching students at this level that they will be potential Reiki teachers and you should teach them accordingly.

Usui Reiki Ryoho

At this level Reiki practitioners need to have a much deeper and more accurate understanding of Usui Reiki Ryoho. This includes the history, the theory and the practice of Reiki. This is an essential element in a Reiki student's progression to becoming a good Reiki master/teacher.

The Gokai

The Gokai or Reiki precepts or ideals need to be understood in a deeper, more enlightened way and integrated into a student's life at this level. This is essential for a master/teacher course.

Reiki lineage

The importance of a Reiki teacher's lineage is explained. This needs to be part of a Reiki course at any level.

Responsibilities Of A Reiki Master/Teacher

As a Reiki master/teacher you are able to attune students into the art of Reiki. This can be a life-changing event for most students, and as a teacher you need to be aware of your responsibilities. This is essential to any Reiki course at this level.

The DKM

The DKM is absolutely essential to this course. The meaning of the DKM needs to be explained. The correct use of the DKM needs to be explained in detail.

21 Day Cleansing Process

A more in-depth analysis of the 21 day cleansing process should be provided.

Reiju Empowerment

Reiju is an essential part of Reiki, even if it is not used to attune students. Knowledge of the Reiju process is an important element that needs to be taught.

Attunement Biofeedback

The sensations or feelings experienced by students when they are attuned need to be understood, as a good Reiki teacher will need to explain these to their students.

Reiki Attunements

The theory of the attunement process needs to be fully explained. The importance of focus and concentration needs to be emphasised.

Practice Giving Reiki Attunements

Sufficient time should be allowed for students to practice giving the attunements. This should not be done on other students but rather on a cuddly toy of some kind or something similar. Students need to have confidence in their ability to give attunements by the end of the course.

Traditional Usui Reiki Techniques

The remainder of the traditional Usui Reiki techniques can be taught at this level. These techniques can be taught at the earlier levels, but we feel that a fair amount of experience of working with energy and self-development is required to use these methods effectively, and this point in a student's Reiki path is pretty much the right level.

Usui Reiki Ryoho Hikkei

This is the companion handbook given to Usui-sensei's students. We discuss and explain the main elements of the Hikkei with students. This is a useful exercise that gives greater insight and understanding of both Reiki and Usui-sensei. The Hikkei gives perspective to Reiki within the context of the culture and era of its initial development.

Teaching Reiki

It is important to teach your students, who are after all potential Reiki teachers, how to teach Reiki in a professional and effective way. This by necessity involves the students developing in areas other than Reiki, such as effective communication, presentation and interpersonal skills.

Recommended Syllabus For Each Level

It is important to teach students a good syllabus for each level they will be teaching. Good knowledge is essential for any Reiki course. By giving recommended syllabuses to your students, every potential Reiki teacher you teach will know precisely what to teach on each level, and will be teaching the best possible knowledge of Reiki in the spirit of Usui-sensei.

Reiki Lineage

Reiki lineage refers to the line of Reiki Masters that leads to the student. For Usui Reiki the line begins with Usui-sensei, and continues with one of his Reiki Masters, and then to one of theirs and so it continues. As far as we are concerned for a healing system to be called Reiki in the recognised sense of the word and be recognized as such, the lineage must trace back to Mikao Usui.

Chapter Twenty Eight

The 21 Day Cleansing Process

The 21 day cleansing process or the Reiki healing crisis as it is sometimes called, is the term used by Reiki practitioners and teachers to describe the healing effects and changes that are experienced by a student when they are attuned to Reiki. These effects can also occur after a single Reiki treatment, but it is more common after a great deal of Reiki treatments.

Some Reiki teachers say the 21 day cleansing process is not actually real. They say that because Reiki masters/teachers tell their students about the effects of the 21 day cleansing process it causes them to 'feel' phantom symptoms. Basically, they believe it is all down to auto-suggestion and that it is fundamentally psychosomatic.

Needless to say this is not correct and shows a lack of understanding not just of Reiki, but of healing in general. Whenever anyone undergoes some kind of healing or detoxification on a physical or even an emotional level there will be some kind of reaction or change. This process of change is the healing effect of Reiki on the physical, emotional and spiritual bodies and will last as long as it lasts - not 21 days as many Reiki practitioners and teachers believe. The length and severity of the symptoms experienced by a student are dependent on a number of factors and are unique to each individual student.

To understand the cleansing process you need to firstly understand the attunement process. The attunements primarily reconnect the student, or enhance their existing connection to the source of the Reiki energy and raise their spiritual frequency. These two factors are the main cause of the 21 day cleansing process. The student's lifestyle, spiritual, emotional and physical well-being dictate the severity of their symptoms.

Once attuned, you will start to have a higher spiritual vibrational frequency, which changes the way you see the world and your place in the world. You now have a higher awareness and are able to see things from a much more Divine perspective. This creates a desire for change, a desire for growth and development. For many people this involves a great deal of soul searching and reflection as they take time to evaluate where they are and what they have achieved so far in their life.

During this time your increased awareness gives you greater insight into your higher path and soul purpose on Earth. You can choose to follow your higher path, which may mean changes to your existing way of life but will ultimately lead to true happiness and fulfilment, or you can choose to carry on as you are. Even though this may feel safe and comfortable, it will not bring about all the necessary changes.

Having this strong connection to the source of the energy means you are receiving Reiki energy constantly, which has a healing effect on your spiritual, emotional and physical bodies. Physically, your body will try to detoxify and heal itself. As with any detoxification process the body expels toxins, causing feelings of upset stomach, diarrhoea, headache and very often tiredness and fatigue. By making healthy changes to your diet and lifestyle the detoxification can be made easier and shorter.

Emotionally, your mind will try to heal any past or present trauma, which can be a painful process in itself. Memories and events long forgotten can come to the surface to be healed away, starting a period of inner reflection and re-evaluation. Sometimes unusual dreams occur, or dreams of past painful or sad events as your mind works through emotional traumas as part of the healing process. These feelings and experiences, though they may be uncomfortable, are part of the recovery process as you return to a more deeply healed state.

As deeper healing takes effect, changes are brought about in your mental, emotional and spiritual life, which in turn lead to changes in your physical life. As your awareness increases, you may discard or change aspects of your life that no longer fit in with your newfound wisdom and knowledge. Every area of your life can be scrutinised and improved, unwanted and irrelevant emotions can dissipate and negative patterns of behaviour can be discarded and replaced with healthier ways. Old ways of thinking are replaced with new innovative ideas. You can find yourself having the confidence to do things you only ever dreamt about before. Associations with people that are damaging to you are severed...and so on.

As with any major reorganisation, it can be a difficult and painful process, but if you allow change to happen when it needs to rather than looking for change, it becomes a subtle and natural period of adjustment. The important thing is to trust your intuition and allow yourself to be guided by your higher self rather than your physical self. Let your awareness grow naturally, then as your awareness grows, allow yourself to change physically and emotionally to match your level of awareness.

For some people this can be a difficult and confusing time, where things seem to be getting worse, however, things will soon settle down, and noticeable improvements will have been made in a physical, emotional, and spiritual sense. It is important to accept what ever happens over this period, it can only be for your highest good. Once the process is complete, you will feel much healthier, happier and lighter. You will be more positive, and be able to see life in a much clearer way. You will have taken another step on your spiritual journey.

By self-healing frequently and regularly, the healing is deeper and more effective, and the cleansing process becomes easier and shorter.

Chapter Twenty Nine

Self-Healing

The Importance Of Self-Healing

For Usui-sensei, Reiki Ryoho was a means to unite the body, mind and spirit to attain enlightenment. Self-healing was, and still is, the most vital part of this process. As you continually self-heal on a daily basis, you become more aware of your self and your place and purpose in the Universe. You heal your physical conditions and your emotional traumas, and you live in a more conscious way, that is with 'right thinking and right living.'.

If you heal yourself enough you get to the point where you love everyone unconditionally, including yourself and you have a profound understanding of the Universe, how it works, why we are all here and what you have to do here. With this awareness comes acceptance that everything that happens to you in life is a blessing because every event was a lesson for you or for someone else. The more healed you are, the better you are as a Reiki healer and teacher and the closer you become to the source of the energy, which many believe to be God or the universe.

Reiki is a wonderful gift, but if you do not use it to heal yourself, you will not make any headway on your higher path, you will not become more spiritual and you will not be a very good Reiki practitioner or teacher. By self-healing you are taking responsibility for yourself and committing to your higher path, to fulfilling your purpose on Earth. As you devote more time to healing yourself you change the way you live your life, you do the things that are right for your higher self, you look after your body, mind and soul and you stop doing the things that are damaging to you.

Usui-sensei was influenced by Japanese Buddhism, which included precepts urging Buddhists to refrain from: stealing, committing adultery, drinking intoxicants, killing, as well as abstaining from certain other activities. As you self-heal you find that to stay on your path you must refrain from certain behaviours and actions. Additionally you will start to live a more holistic lifestyle. This is not a forced and difficult process but one that occurs naturally and quite simply. This enables you to be a good Reiki healer, a good teacher and places you further along your higher path.

Unfortunately there are some Reiki practitioners and teachers who do not emphasise the importance of self-healing and rarely self heal themselves. Some teach that you only need to self-heal during the first twenty-one days of your Reiki journey (the 21 day cleansing process). Purely healing others all the time does not bring you closer to enlightenment, raise your frequency or heal you. It's like the blind leading the blind. How can Reiki practitioners or teachers help someone else if they have not been helping themselves? Usui-sensei makes this point himself in the Usui Reiki Hikkei (Usui Reiki Handbook) saying "if you can't heal yourself, how can you heal others." The time you spend healing yourself helps you to develop a profound understanding of how the energy works.

When you self-heal your awareness grows and you cannot plead ignorance in the face of your actions. For example, if before you did Reiki you used to smoke fifty cigarettes a day and after learning Reiki your intuition told you, this is killing you, you must quit, then you have to quit. The reason for this being that you are in a state of awareness and as an aware person you cannot justify doing something that is damaging to yourself and to God or the Universe whom you are part of.

Of course you have the choice of ignoring your intuition, but if you do so, you must then accept that the consequences will be harsher than they would have been before you learned Reiki because you have deliberately gone out of your way to ignore your intuition. So it goes, the more you self heal, in effect, the less you can do, in terms of pursuing physical desires and wants.

However, you gain so much more spiritually and in so many other ways too. No sacrifice you make with Reiki is ever really a sacrifice, but a wonderful gift. Self-healing leads to happiness as you accept your path, trust your intuition and develop an unshakable faith in God or the Universe. Usui-sensei said that as you become healed on all levels, physical, emotional and spiritual you are "able to live a happy life and heal others with God's energy." We would all be wise to follow his example.

Self-Healing

As a Reiki practitioner or teacher you should be self-healing on a daily basis. You need to make Reiki an integral part of your life. Reiki should be something that you look forward to and something you would not want to do without. You should start from your level 1 course and self-heal with the high frequency Rei energy on a spiritual level. You should be doing at least two self-healings each day, but more would be better. You should treat yourself using the main hand-positions to ensure you are receiving healing in a balanced and complete way.

After a period of self-healing with the Rei energy you should then start to heal with the CKR energy to treat your physical body and the SHK energy to treat your emotional body. You should again be treating yourself at least twice each and every day. Obviously, the more you can self-heal the better it is for you. Again you should be using all the main hand-positions to give an overall balanced healing, but you should also treat specific areas that you feel need additional healing. You can do this through intuition or guidance or by feeling the flow of energy or by simply knowing your body.

As well as self-healing in this way, you can work any conditions you may have or pick up at any time, whether they are physical illnesses or injuries or emotional trauma.

NB: Always remember to see a clinician if you have any illnesses or injuries. Reiki is not a substitute for qualified medical care.

Chapter Thirty

Law and Regulation

The Law Regarding Reiki

There are specific laws to regulate and govern the practice of complementary therapists in every country. This is something that should be taught on every Reiki course to ensure Reiki practitioners work within the law.

Why The Practice And Teaching Of Reiki Should Be Regulated

There are many reasons why we believe the teaching and practice of Reiki needs to be regulated. Quite a number of Reiki practitioners and teachers disagree with us on this issue, as they do on many other aspects of Reiki.

We can see why some Reiki people see regulation as an interference, an unnecessary intrusion into their freedom to teach and practice Reiki as they wish to, but Usui Reiki Ryoho does not belong to them, it is not their system, they did not discover or develop it. They should have respect for the founder and his teachings and should therefore endeavour to practice and teach his methods in his prescribed way. They should also have respect for their clients and students and offer them the service they are paying for.

Any changes a Reiki teacher introduces to the original system should be taught as add-ons so students know what is original Usui Reiki Ryoho and what is a modern addition introduced by the teacher or their teacher or their teacher before them. As an example, many Reiki teachers now teach that Reiki is based on the chakra system and teach all about chakras and how to heal them. The fact that Reiki is not based on the chakra system seems to have totally eluded them.

The chakra system is an Indian view of the body's energy system. It is not a Japanese view of the energy system, and is definitely not a part Usui Reiki Ryoho. Things like this detract from the system Usui-sensei developed and cause confusion amongst both students and teachers.

By having some kind of regulation we can ensure that every Usui Reiki course being taught will at the very least include a standardised core curriculum that teaches the basic minimum knowledge and techniques that will allow any student to practice Reiki effectively and safely.

The other aspect of regulation that is essential is the protection of clients and students against poor practice and unscrupulous practitioners. We know the vast majority of Reiki practitioners and teachers, whether they are working professionally or just using Reiki for themselves and friends and family, are both genuine and sincere about their use of Reiki. Unfortunately, no matter how well intentioned the practitioner or teacher is, if they have been taught to practice in a way that is ineffective or even harmful, then that will be the outcome, an ineffective treatment or a treatment that leaves the client feeling worse than before.

Obviously, there are in the Reiki profession, as there are in any other, a few practitioners and teachers that will abuse their position, especially since in many cases they are working with vulnerable people. We need to have regulations in place to try to minimise the risks to clients and students from both. How this is achieved is the difficulty, striking a balance between protecting clients and students and protecting the freedom of the Reiki practitioners and teachers.

What we would like to see is a Reiki governing body that will issue guidelines for both teaching and healing that can include best practice from across the range of Reiki styles as well as the teachings of Usui-sensei. At the heart of regulation needs to be a set core curriculum that teaches not only the best available knowledge and techniques for Usui Reiki Ryoho but guidelines on working safely, effectively and professionally with clients.

Chapter Thirty One

Responsibility

Teaching Reiki

As a Reiki teacher, you are able to attune students to the Reiki energy by connecting them to the source of the energy - to God (or the Universe). For some Reiki teachers this is all they need to do on a Reiki course or workshop, for others it is enough to add some very basic Reiki techniques. This is not the way to teach Usui Reiki Ryoho. Usui-sensei taught Reiki with a great deal of knowledge, as well as the healing methods and meditations.

The shirushi (symbols) are an essential part of Usui Reiki Ryoho, and need to be taught to all students. The use of the shirushi and their corresponding jumon (name) and kotodama (mantra) are used to connect to and access the various frequencies of energy. This process needs to be carried out with a high level of accuracy as any changes in the shirushi, jumon or kotodama can change the frequency of the energy being channelled.

The Gokai (Reiki precepts) are an important element of Reiki that needs to be explained to students. The concept of right thinking, right living and self-healing needs to be impressed on students. Only by this means can a student develop and fulfil their potential on Earth and reach enlightenment.

Today, as teachers we need to teach Reiki in a professional way to ensure our students have the knowledge and ability to treat clients effectively and safely, and once they become Reiki teachers, to teach students themselves to the required standard. By dong this, we can make Reiki more acceptable and therefore more accessible to the general public and to the medical profession.

The Reiki syllabuses we have discussed in previous chapters give a complete course structure for the first four levels of Usui Reiki Ryoho. As a Reiki teacher you not only need to fully understand the underpinning knowledge of Reiki, but the energy you are working with too, which only comes with regular self-healing and with healing others.

The level 1, 2, 3, 4 and 5 courses are really one course that Usui-sensei originally taught as an ongoing training path, similar to a martial arts path. This path was later split into separate levels to make it easier for students to learn. Level 1 and 2 should be taught as one course, either together or with a short interval, as together they teach basic Reiki Ryoho. The knowledge and ability gained on the level 1 and 2 course allows the student to heal themselves and others on a spiritual, emotional and physical level and to start their spiritual journey.

There needs to be a gap between level 2 and 3 and between level 3 and 4 to allow the student to develop their healing ability, to move forward on their spiritual journey and to reach the required level of development. This gap cannot be quantified as a general timescale, but needs to be based on each individual's level. As a Reiki master you need to be able to assess each individual with regards to their knowledge and understanding of Reiki and their practical ability of working with the Reiki energy. You should teach the higher levels of Reiki to students that are ready for those levels.

By teaching these syllabuses you give your students the best possible foundation to grow from and can ensure they will have a deep understanding of Usui Reiki Ryoho, its underpinning knowledge and its practices. Students will be able to develop spiritually and effectively heal themselves and their clients in a safe and professional manner.

We should continue Usui-sensei's legacy of sharing and spreading Reiki in society to share the gift with as many people as we can, with the aim of improving society.

Taking Responsibility As A Reiki Practitioner Or Teacher

What does 'taking responsibility' mean? Teaching Reiki and giving Reiki treatments carries with it responsibilities and obligations to Usui-sensei and to the students and clients.

When teaching a Reiki course, we have an obligation to the founder of Reiki to teach his method in his spirit and with his teachings to the best of our ability. This in practice means ensuring we have researched and found out as much as we can about Usui-sensei's teachings. It means we have worked with the methods and techniques of Reiki daily to become proficient and to truly understand Reiki. It means we have healed ourselves and developed and grown spiritually to teach with intuition and awareness. Only in this way can we truly teach Usui Reiki Ryoho.

When we treat clients we have a responsibility to treat them safely, effectively and professionally. We should work to heal their conditions, whether they are physical or emotional or both. This means we work on the presenting symptom(s) with the type and frequency of energy that will have the greatest healing effect on the symptom(s). It means we use effective intentions and visualisations to further increase the healing effects of the energy. It means we stay focused when we are healing and concentrate on our healing work.

Moving Reiki Into The Mainstream

Many people nowadays have heard of Reiki or know someone who practices Reiki. The problem is too many people don't know what Reiki is and if they do have some idea of how this therapy works, it is often a poor idea generated by the general lack of knowledge amongst the Reiki community at large about how Reiki works.

Often Reiki is seen as a 'flaky' spiritual healing art that has no real scientific or logical grounding and at best provides a nice relaxation treatment for the receiver. This unfortunately is the overriding perception of Reiki, not only amongst the public in general but amongst the medical profession too. This poses a massive obstacle to the acceptance of Reiki as a complementary therapy that doctors can refer patients to.

Reiki is so much more than this. Reiki works directly on any condition. Usui-sensei said himself in the Usui Reiki Hikkei (Usui Reiki handbook), that any physical or emotional illness could be cured by the Usui system of natural healing. Somewhere this got lost amongst the mumblings of the many teachers who changed Usui-sensei's teachings. Someone somewhere came up with the outlandish idea that Reiki energy is intelligent enough to know exactly where and what to treat in each individual client and that it will go exactly where the body requires it. If this is the case why does a healer need to channel the energy into someone at all? Surely if the energy goes where it needs to go we can all just lie back and say "Reiki energy heal me now" and it will be done. This is preposterous. The energy goes where the healer puts it. If you heal someone's foot the energy will go there. Eventually it may work its way up the leg and the rest of the body but by the time it's done that the person will probably have developed a new condition.

Reiki needs to be grounded in more logic and viewed seriously as a complementary therapy, with the same sort of status as acupuncture or herbal medicine. We need doctors and the rest of the medical profession to take Reiki seriously and for them to do that we cannot go around talking about energy exchanges and intelligent energy doing the work by itself. We need to understand that every part of the body will respond to precise frequencies of energy to initiate and enhance the repair and regeneration process and if we channel the correct frequency into a damaged part of the body, we can restore the body to optimum health.

Reiki can be both spiritual and clinical at the same time. Waving crystal wands, tinkling bells and holding hands and singing is not going to cure the world of its ills. We need to work within the boundaries we have been set by the government and set our own high quality, clinical standards for Reiki and not the minimum standards that most Reiki practitioners are happy to grit their teeth and bear.

We need foresight. If we have minimum standards for Reiki and then a bad practitioner abuses their position, the whole of Reiki will be discredited. A good Reiki practitioner should always take responsibility for their work if Reiki is to be taken seriously as a complementary therapy by healthcare professionals.

There are Reiki practitioners that work voluntarily within the National Health Service (NHS) in the United Kingdom. Angie Buxton-King is a well-known practitioner who has written a book about her experience working as a fulltime paid healer at University College Hospital, London. This is wonderful and hopefully more Reiki healers will he employed by the NHS in the UK and in health services around the world. However the right sort of Reiki needs to be used. If Reiki healers are working within the health service, they should be using comprehensive interview and treatment forms and at the very least promoting working directly on physical and emotional conditions. It would be wonderful if we could show the medical profession that not only is Reiki a wonderful stress reliever and peace promoter but an actual physical therapy that can work directly on healing any condition.

Usui-sensei said himself that Reiki is the 'miraculous medicine of all diseases' and is simple to learn and practice. It also states on Usui-sensei's memorial stone that he cured many people. We need to get rid of some of the mystery and magic people have whisked around Reiki and show that Reiki is a grounded and clinical therapy as well as a wonderful spiritual journey for those who choose to take that route.

The Way Forward For Reiki Healing

Usui-sensei's greatest goal was to spread Reiki to as many people as possible during his lifetime. Unfortunately, after he died, the society he founded to continue his teachings (Usui Reiki Ryoho Gakkai) became very closed and secretive. There were many students of Usui-sensei that started their own schools of Reiki healing throughout Japan and spread their own teachings. Outside of Japan there are many Reiki teachers spreading their own versions of Reiki to many people worldwide. Ideally what we need is for the Usui Reiki Ryoho Gakkai to allow the knowledge of Usui-sensei's teachings to be spread beyond their membership.

By sharing the original teachings of Usui-sensei, the Gakkai can help to standardise Reiki in a form similar to Usui-sensei's original Reiki Ryoho. At least in this way, anyone that wants to learn traditional Reiki can do so and be assured that it is true to the original.

The other forms of Reiki in existence today we believe will never revert back to the original. There seems to be a feeling among many Reiki teachers that have developed their own form of Reiki that 'their' system of Reiki is somehow better or more effective or has new and more powerful energy connections...etc. For them going back to Usui-sensei's original Reiki Ryoho would be a step backwards. We do not think we will be able to ever bring together the different forms of Reiki into one effective and practical method.

So we are left with those of us that want to practice Reiki as closely as we can in the way of Usui-sensei, and those that believe Reiki should change and evolve into newer and better incarnations. However we choose to practice Reiki, some things should be common to all of us. We should work in a professional and ethical way. Our aim should be to develop ourselves through self-healing and 'right thinking and right living'. We should use our Reiki to help others as much as we can, and if we choose to work as Reiki therapists we should use and promote Reiki as a healing therapy that can work on any condition. By setting high standards for ourselves we can establish Reiki as a true complementary therapy that can be used alongside Western medicine to treat any condition effectively.

Chapter Thirty Two

Conclusion

The Essence Of Usui Reiki Ryoho

What is the essence of Usui Reiki Ryoho? Is the essence of Usui Reiki Ryoho in the theory, or in the practice, or in the way of life that Usui-sensei proscribed? The essence of Reiki lies in the spirit with which Usui-sensei approached not only Reiki but life as well. How do we teach Reiki in the spirit of Usui-sensei? How do we continue the work that Usui-sensei started?

With the limited information we have available to us at the moment regarding Usui-sensei's teachings, some of which pre-dates his Reiki teachings, we cannot possibly hope to teach Reiki exactly as Usui-sensei did, we simply do not have enough of his syllabus to do that. Sure, we know much of the theory and many of the techniques and methods now, but still not quite the complete system. We know a little about Usui-sensei's life, we know a little about Usui-sensei the man but again, how much do we really know and how much is speculation and inference? We think that much of what is known of the teachings of Usui-sensei and of the man himself has been interpreted and in some cases interpreted badly, and inferences and changes have been made that detract from the original meaning and purpose.

To teach Usui Reiki in the true spirit of Usui-sensei we need to understand Usui-sensei as a man and as a teacher. We are able to construct a picture of the man through his words and his deeds. We can have an appreciation of the man through his legacy and the words of his students. The fact that Usui-sensei was dedicated to the improvement of mind, body and soul is beyond question, it is common knowledge that he worked tirelessly throughout his life to develop and improve himself. We are certain that he lived his life as he taught others to live theirs, through 'right thinking and right living'. We know that he taught his methods widely to make individuals better for themselves and for the good of society as a whole. We understand that he went against the normal expectations of his culture to spread his teachings freely. We know that his system of healing, his beloved Reiki Ryoho, was a path to enlightenment. And above all we know that he used his Reiki Ryoho to treat and to cure people suffering from physical injuries and chronic illnesses as well as people with mental and emotional illnesses.

We are able to use his Reiki Ryoho in the spirit in which he intended by working in an active way with the energy to try our best to heal every client that comes to us. We can practice our Reiki in a conscious and focused way so that we too can follow in the original path. We should adhere to the processes and rituals of each technique as exactly as we can because we know that every part, every detail, however small or insignificant it may appear to us when we first start, has a specific and essential purpose which becomes obvious once we reach a higher level of understanding. We should work hard to develop and improve ourselves through self-healing with Reiki and through understanding and following the Gokai (Reiki precepts). We can respect Usui-sensei and his teachings and stop trying to improve or adapt or change or re-interpret his system for financial gain or to boost our egos or status. We can simply practice Reiki with honesty and love to the best of our ability.

Ultimately the true spirit of Usui Reiki Ryoho lies within us as Reiki teachers and practitioners in the way we live our lives, and in the way we practice Usui-sensei's teachings. Today, we can follow his teachings and we can live our lives as he taught and as he lived his life. In this way we can teach and practice Usui Reiki in the true spirit of the founder Mikao Usui.

"The secret method of inviting happiness
The miraculous medicine of all diseases

Just for today, do not anger
Do not worry and be filled with gratitude
Devote yourself to your work and be kind to people

Every morning and evening join your hands in prayer, pray these words
to your heart and chant these words with your mouth
Usui Reiki Treatment for the improvement of body and mind"

Usui, Makao, Founder of Usui Reiki Ryoho

SECTION SIX

END NOTES

References

1. Usui Memorial stone inscription

2. Stiene, Bronwen and Frans. The Reiki Source Book, O Books, Winchester (UK), New York (USA) 2003

3. Rand, William Lee. Reiki The Healing Touch, Vision Publications, Southfield (USA) 2000

4. Petter, Frank Arjava. The Original Reiki Handbook, Lotus Press Twin Lakes (USA) 1999

5. Usui Reiki Ryoho Hikkei © Universal copyright Richard R. Rivard, B.Sc. Reiki Master/Teacher - www.threshold.ca

6. Liboff AR. 1994, The electromagnetic field as a biological variable. In: Frey AH (ed.) On the Nature of Electromagnetic Field Interactions. Austin: R.G. Landis.

7. Seto A, Kusaka C, Nakazato S et al 1992 Detection of extraordinary large biomagnetic field strength from human hands. Acupuncture and Electro-Therapeutics Research International Journal 17:75-94

8. Zimmerman J, 1990 Laying-on-of hands healing and Therapeutic Touch: a testable theory. BEMI Currents, Journal of the Bioelectromagnetics Institute 2:8-17

9. Choi C., Hoo W.M., Lee M.B., Yang J.S., Soh K.-S., Yang J.S., Yoon G., Kim M., Zaslawsky C. and Chang J.J. 2002 Biophoton

Emission from the Hands. Journal of the Korean Physical Society, August 2002 Vol. 41, No. 2, pp. 275_278

10. Schwartz S A, DeMattei R J, Brame K G, Spottiswoode S J P 1990 Infrared spectra alteration in water proximate to the palms of therapeutic practitioners. Subtle Energies 1:43-72

11. Chien C-H, Tsuei J.J, Lee S C Huang Y-C, Wei Y-H 1991 Effect of emmited bioenergy on biomechanical functions of cells. American Journal of Chinese Medicine 19:285-293

12. Sisken B F, Walker J 1995 Therapeutic aspects of electromagnetic fields for soft-tissue healing. In: Blank M (ed) Electromagnetic fields: biological interactions and mechanisms. Advances in Chemistry Series 250. American Chemical Society, Washington DC pp 277-285

13. Bassett, C.A.L., Pawluk, R.J., Pilla, A.A. (1974) Acceleration of Fracture Repair by Electromagnetic Fields. Ann NY Acad Sci. 238:242-262.

14. Bassett, C.A.L., Pilla, A.A., Pawluk, R. (1977) A non-surgical salvage of surgically-resistant pseudoarthroses and non-unions by pulsing electromagnetic fields. Clin Orthop 124:117-131.

15. Goodman R, Bassett CAL, Henderson AS. 1983 Pulsing electromagnetic fields induce cellular transcription. Science 1983;220:1283–1285.

16. Goodman R, Blank M. 2002. Insights into electromagnetic interaction mechanisms. J Cell Physiol 2002;192:16–22.

17. Marko S. Markov 2007 Pulsed electromagnetic field therapy

history, state of the art and future. The Environmentalist – DOI10.1007/s10669-007-9128-2

18. Pilla, A.A. 1972 Electrochemical information and energy transfer in vivo. Proc. 7th IECEC, Washington, D.C., American Chemical Society. 761-64.

19. Pilla, A.A. 1974 Electrochemical Information Transfer at Living Cell Membranes. Ann NY Acad Sci, 238:149-170.

20. Pilla, A.A., Muehsam, D.J., Markov, M.S. 1997 A dynamical systems/Larmor precession model for weak magnetic field bioeffects: Ion-binding and orientation of bound water molecules. Bioelectrochem Bioenergetics 43:239-249.

21. Liboff, A.R. 1985 Cyclotron resonance in membrane transport. In: Chiabrera, A., Nicolini, C., Schwan, H.P., eds. Interactions between in Interactions Between Electromagnetic Fields and Cells. Plenum Press, New York. 281-396.

22. Liboff, A.F., Fozek, R.J., Sherman, M.L., McLeod. B.R., Smith, S.D. 1987 Ca2+-45 cyclotron resonance in human lymphocytes. J Bioelectricity 6:13–22.

23. Diebert MC, McLeod BR, Smith SD, Liboff AR. 1994, Ion resonance electromagnetic field stimulation of fracture healing in rabbits with a fibular ostectomy. J Orthop Res 1994;12:878–885.

24. Bianco, B., Chiabrera, A. (1992) From the Langevin-Lorentz to the Zeeman model of electromagnetic effects on ligand-receptor binding. Bioelectrochem Bioenergetics. 28:355-365.

25. Lednev, V.V. 1991 Possible mechanism for the influence of

weak magnetic fields on biological systems. Bioelectromagnetics 12:71-75.

26. Blanchard, J.P., Blackman, C.F. (1994) Clarification and application of an ion parametric resonance model for magnetic field interactions with biological systems. Bioelectromagnetics 15:217-238.

27. Blackman, C.F., Blanchard, J.P., Benane, S.G., House, D.E. 1995 The ion parametric resonance model predicts magnetic field parameters that affect nerve cells. FASEB J. 9:547-51.

28. Engstrom, S. 1996 Dynamic properties of Lednev's parametric resonance mechanism. Bioelectromagnetics 17:58-70.

29. Shuvalova, L.A., Ostrovskaya, M.V., Sosunov, E.A., Lednev, V.V. 1991 Weak magnetic field influence of the speed of calmodulin dependent phosphorylation of myosin in solution. Dokladi Acad Nauk USSR 217: 227.

30. Markov, M.S., Ryaby, J.T., Kaufman, J.J., Pilla, A.A. 1992 Extremely weak AC and DC magnetic field significantly affect myosin phosphorylation. In: Allen, M.J., Cleary, S.F., Sowers, A.E., Shillady D.D., eds. Charge and Field Effects in Biosystems-3, Birkhauser, Boston 1992; 225-230

31. Markov, M.S., Wang, S., Pilla, A.A. 1993 Effects of weak low frequency sinusoidal and DC magnetic fields on myosin phosphorylation in a cell-free preparation. Bioelectrochem Bioenergetics 30:119-125.

32. Markov, M.S., Muehsam, D.J., Pilla, A.A. 1994 Modulation of Cell-Free Myosin Phosphorylation with Pulsed Radio Frequency Electromagnetic Fields. In Allen, M.J., Cleary, S.F,

Sowers, A.E., eds. Charge and Field Effects in Biosystems 4. World Scientific, New Jersey. 274-288.

33. Markov, M.S., Pilla, A.A. 1993 Ambient range sinusoidal and DC magnetic fields affect myosin phosphorylation in a cell-free preparation. In: Blank, M., ed. Electricity and Magnetism in Biology and Medicine. San Francisco Press. 323-327.

34. Markov, M.S., Pilla, A.A. 1994 Static magnetic field modulation of myosin phosphorylation: Calcium dependence in two enzyme preparations. Bioelectrochem. Bioenergetics. 35:57-61.

35. Markov, M.S., Pilla, A.A. 1994 Modulation of Cell-Free Myosin Light Chain Phosphorylation with Weak Low Frequency and Static Magnetic Fields. In: Frey, A., ed. On the Nature of Electromagnetic Field Interactions with Biological Systems. R.G. Landes Co., Austin. 127-141.

36. Liburdy, R.P., Yost, M.G. 1993 Tme-varying and static magnetic fields act in combination to alter calcium signal transduction in the lymphocyte. In: Blank, M., ed. Electricity and Magnetism in Biology and Medicine. San Francisco Press 331-334.

37. Engstrom, S., Markov, M.S., McLean, M.J., Holcomb, R.R., Markov, J.M. 2002 Effects of non-uniform static magnetic fields on the rate of myosin phosphorylation. Bioelectromagnetics 23:475-479.

38. Liboff, A.R., Cherng, S., Jenrow, K.A., Bull, A. 2003 Calmodulin-dependent cyclic nucleotide phosphodiesterase activity is altered by 20 mT magnetostatic fields. Bioelectromagnetics 24:32-38.

39. Blank M. 1995a. Electromagnetic fields: biological interactions and mechanisms. Washington DC: American Chemical Soc. 498 p.

40. Blank M. 1995b. Na/K-adenosine-triphosphatase. Adv Chem 250:339–348.

41. Blank M, Soo L. 1998. Enhancement of cytochrome oxidase activity in 60 Hz magnetic fields. Bioelectrochem Bioenerg 45:253–259.

42. Goodman R, Blank M. 1998. Magnetic field stress induces expression of hsp70. Cell Stress Chap 3:74–88.

43. Blank M, Goodman R. 1999. Electromagnetic fields may act directly on DNA. J Cell Biochem 15:369–374.

44. Blank M, Goodman R. 2001. Electromagnetic initiation of transcription at specific DNA sites. J Cell Biochem 81:689–692.

45. Canaday, D.J., Lee, R.C. 1991 Scientific basis for clinical applications of electric fields in soft-tissue repair. In: Brighton, C.T., Pollack, S.R., eds. Electromagnetics in Biology and Medicine, San Francisco Press Inc., 1991: 275-291

46. Lee, R.C., Canaday, D.J/, Doong, H. 1993 A review of the biophysical basis for the clinical application of electric fields in soft-tissue repair. J Burn Care Rehabil 14:319-335.

47. Jenkins L.S.; Duerstock B.S.; Borgens R.B. September 1996 Reduction of the current of injury leaving the amputation inhibits limb regeneration in the Red Spotted Newt. Developmental Biology, Volume 178, Number 2, pp. 251-262(12)

48. Becker, R. O., 1972, Electrical stimulation of partial limb regeneration in mammals, Bulletin of the New York Academy of Medicine, 2nd series, 48, 627-641.

49. Becker, R. O., 1972, Stimulation of partial limb regeneration in rats. Nature, 235, 109-111.

50. Smith SD. 1967, Induction of partial limb regeneration in Rana pipiens by galvanic stimulation. Anat Rec; 158:89–98.

51. Nordenstron BEW. 1983 Biologically Closed Electric Circuits. Stockholm: Nordic Medical Publications.

52. Chou CK. 1997 Electrochemical treatment of tumor. Bioelectromagnetics 18:1.

53. Xin Y-L, Xue F-Z, Ge B-S, Zhao F-R, Shi B, Zhang W. 1997 Electrochemical treatment of lung cancer. Bioelectromagnetics 18:8–13.

54. Fröhlich H 1968 Bose condensation of strongly excited longitudinal electric modes. Physics Letters 26A:402-403

55. Fröhlich H 1988 Biological coherence and response to external stimuli. Springer Verlag, Berlin

56. Ingber, D.E. and Folkman, J. 1989a. Tension and compression as basic determinants of cell form and function: utilization of a cellular tensegrity mechanism. In Cell Shape: Determinants, Regulation and Regulatory Role (ed. Stein, W. and Bronner, F.), pp. 1-32. Academic Press: Orlando, FL.

57. Ingber, D.E. and Folkman, J. 1989b. Mechanochemical switching between growth and differentiation during

fibroblast growth factor-stimulated angiogenesis in vitro: role of extracellular matrix. J. Cell Biol. 109, 317-330.

58. Fuller, B. 1961 Tensegrity. Portfolio Artnews Annual 4, 112-127.

59. Pienta KJ, Coffey DS 1991 Cellular harmonic information transfer through a tissue tensegrity matrix system. Medical Hypotheses 34:88-95

60. Theise N. D.and Bushell W. C. From the global to the local: Possible pathways for the transduction of Indo-Sino-Tibetan cognitive-behavioural practices into site specific, tissue regenerative effects. In Press.

61. Bushell WC, 2005a. Model: Potential cognitive-behavioral stem cell activation in multiple niches. Presented at the "Stem Cell Biology & Human Disease" conference (UCSD/Salk Institute/Nature Medicine), La Jolla CA, March 17-19, 2005.

62. Abbasoglu O et al., 1995. The effect of the pineal gland on liver regeneration in rats, J Hepatology 23: 578-81.

63. Esrefoglu M et al., 2005. Potent therapeutic effect of melatonin on aging skin in pinealectomized rats, J Pineal Research 39(3): 231-7.

64. Kobayashi H, et al., 2005. A role of melatonin in neuroectodermal-mesodermal interactions: the hair follicle synthesizes melatonin and expresses functional melatonin receptors. FASEB J. 2005 Oct;19(12):1710-2.

65. Slominski A, et al., 2005. On the role of melatonin in skin physiology and pathology. Endocrine. 2005 Jul 27 (2):137-48.

66. Feng Z et al., 2006. Early melatonin supplementation alleviates oxidative stress in a transgenic mouse model of Alzheimer's disease, Free Radicals in Biology & Medicine 40(1): 101-9.

67. Dundar K et al., 2005. Protective effects of exogenously administered or endogenously produced melatonin on hyperbaric oxygen-induced oxidative stress in the rat brain, Clinical & Experimental Pharmacology and Physiology 32(11): 926-30.

68. Yi C et al., 2005. Effects of melatonin in age-related macular degeneration, Annals of the NY Academy of Sciences 1057: 384-91.

69. Girotti L et al., 2003. Low urinary 6-sulfatoxymelatonin levels in patients with severe congestive heart failure, Endocrine 22(3): 245-8.

70. Castagnino HE et al., 2002. Cytoprotection by melatonin and growth hormone in early rat myocardial infarction as revealed by Feulgen DNA staining, Neurology Endocrinology Letters 23(5-6): 391-5.

71. Bubenik GA, 2002. Gastrointestinal melatonin: localization, function, and clinical relevance, Digestive Disease Science 47: 2336-48.

72. Bellipanni G et al., 2005. Effects of melatonin in perimenopausal and menopausal women: our personal experience, Annals of the NY Academy of Sciences 1057: 393-402

73. Erkanli K et al., 2005. Melatonin protects against ischemia/reperfusion injury in skeletal muscle, J Pineal

Research 39(3): 238-42.

74. Escames G et al., 2006. Melatonin counteracts inducible mitochondrial nitric oxide synthase dependent mitochondrial dysfunction in skeletal muscle of septic mice, J Pineal Research 40(1): 71-8.

75. Reiter RJ et al, 1998. Reactive oxygen intermediates, molecular damage, and aging. Relation to melatonin, Annals of the New York Academy of Sciences 854: 410-24

76. Sainz RM et al, 2003. Melatonin and cell death: differential actions on normal and cancer cells, Cellular & Molecular Life Science 60: 1407-26.

77. Wolfler A et al, 2001. Prooxidant activity of melatonin promotes fas-induced cell death in human leukemic Jurkat cells, FEBS Letters 502: 127-31.

78. Karasek M, 2004. Melatonin, human aging, and age-related diseases, Experimental Gerontology 39(11-12): 1723-9.

79. Ader, R. & Cohen, N. 1975 Behaviorally conditioned immuno-suppression. Psychosom. Med, 1975; 37: 333-340.

80. Rein G., Ph.D. October 1996 Effect of conscious intention on human DNA. Proceeds of the International Forum on New Science, Denver, CO.

81. McCraty R., Ph.D. Atkinson M., and Tomasino D., B.A. 2003 Modulation of DNA conformation by heart-focused intention Institute of HeartMath, Publication No. 03-008. Boulder Creek, CA.

Further Resources

Studies Into EM Fields And Healing

Abeed R.I., Naseer M., and Abel E.W. 1998 Capacitively coupled electrical stimulation treatment: results from patients with failed long bone fracture unions. J. Orthop. Trauma 12, 510-513

Adey W. Ross 2004 Potential therapeutic application of nonthermal electromagnetic fields: Ensemble organization of cells in tissue as a factor in biological field sensing – in Bioelectromagnetic Medicine – Marcel Dekker, NY 1-15

Baker L.L., Chambers R., DeMuth S.K., and Villar F. 1997 Effects of electrical stimulation on wound healing in patients with diabetic ulcers. Diabetes Care 20, 405-412.

Bassett C.A., Becker R.O., Brighton C.T., Lavine L., and Rowley B.A. 1974, Panel discussion: To what extent can electrical stimulation be used in the treatment of human disorders? Ann. N. Y. Acad. Sci. 238, 586-593.

Bassett CA. 1993, Beneficial effects of electromagnetic fields. J Cell Biochem 1993; 51(4): 387-393.

Biedebach M.C. 1989 Accelerated healing of skin ulcers by electrical stimulation and the intracellular physiological mechanisms involved. Acupunct. Electrother. Res. 14, 43-60.

Bilotta TW. The use of low-frequency, low-magnitude PEMFs in treatment of osteoporosis. J Bioelectr 1989; 8(2): 316.

Brighton C.T., Hozack W.J., Brager M.D., Windsor R.E., Pollack

S.R., Vreslovic E.J., and Kotwick J.E. 1985 Fracture healing in the rabbit fibula when subjected to various capacitively coupled electrical fields. J. Orthop. Res. 3, 331-340.

Castillo E., Sumano H., Fortoul T.I., and Zepeda A. 1995 The influence of pulsed electrical stimulation on the wound healing of burned rat skin. Arch. Med. Res. 26, 185-189.

Chang W.H., Hwang I.M., and Liu H.C. 1991 Enhancement of fracture healing by specific pulsed capacitively-coupled electric field stimulation. Front Med. Biol. Eng 3, 57-64.

Cho M.R., Thatte H.S., Lee R.C., and Golan D.E. 2000 Integrin-dependent human macrophage migration induced by oscillatory electrical stimulation. Ann. Biomed. Eng 28, 234-243.

de Haas W.G., Watson J., and Morrison D.M. 1980 Non-invasive treatment of ununited fractures of the tibia using electrical stimulation. J. Bone Joint Surg. Br. 62-B, 465-470.

Feedar J.A., Kloth L.C., and Gentzkow G.D. 1991 Chronic dermal ulcer healing enhanced with monophasic pulsed electrical stimulation. Phys. Ther. 71, 639-649.

Fisher D.A., Rapp G.F., and Emkes M. 1987 Idiopathic scoliosis: transcutaneous muscle stimulation versus the Milwaukee brace. Spine 12, 987-991.

Frank C., Schachar N., Dittrich D., Shrive N., deHaas W., and Edwards G. (1983) Electromagnetic stimulation of ligament healing in rabbits. Clin. Orthop. 263-272.

Gardner S.E., Frantz R.A., and Schmidt F.L. 1999 Effect of electrical stimulation on chronic wound healing: a meta- analysis. Wound.

Repair Regen. 7, 495-503.

Gentzkow G.D. and Miller K.H. 1991 Electrical stimulation for dermal wound healing. Clin. Podiatr. Med. Surg. 8, 827-841.

Herbert M.A. and Bobechko W.P. 1987 Paraspinal muscle stimulation for the treatment of idiopathic scoliosis in children. Orthopedics 10, 1125-1132.

Kirkcaldie MT. 1997 Transcranial magnetic stimulation as therapy for depression and other disorders. Aust N Z J Psychiatry 1997; 31(2): 264-272.

Lee RC, Canaday DJ, Doong H. 1993 A review of the biophysical basis for the clinical application of electric fields in soft tissue repair. J Burn Care Rehab 1993; 14: 319.

Lubennikov VA. 1995 First experience in using a whole-body magnetic field exposure in treating cancer patients. Vopr Onkol 1995; 41(2): 140-141.

MacGinitie L.A., Wu D.D., and Cochran G.V. 1993 Streaming potentials in healing, remodeling, and intact cortical bone. J. Bone Miner. Res. 8, 1323-1335.

Paterson D.C., Hillier T.M., Carter R.F., Ludbrook J., Maxwell G.M., and Savage J.P. 1977 Experiemtnal delayed union of the dog tibia and its use in assessing the effect of an electrical bone growth stimulator. Clin. Orthop. 340-350.

Pilla AA, Kloth L. 1997 Effect of pulsed radio frequency therapy on edema in ankle sprains: a multisite double-blind clinical study. Second World Congress for Electricity and Magnetism in Biology and Magnetism, 8-13 June 1997, Bologna, Italy, p. 300.

Rubik B, Pavek R, Ward R, Greene E, Upledger J, Lawrence D, Ramsden E. 1994 Manual healing methods. NIH Publication No. 94-066. In: Alternative Medicine: Expanding Medical Horizons. Washington, DC: U.S. Government Printing Office, 1994a; 134-157.

Rubik B, Becker RO, Flower RG, Hazlewood CF, Liboff AR, Walleczek J. 1994 Bioelectromagnetics applications in medicine. NIH Publication No. 94-066. In: Alternative Medicine: Expanding Medical Horizons. Washington, DC: U.S. Government Printing Office, 1994b; 45-65.

Salzberg CA. 1995 The effects of non-thermal pulsed electromagnetic energy on wound healing of pressure ulcers in spinal-cord injured patients: a randomized, double-blind study. Ostomy Wound Manage 1995; 41(3): 42-51.

Sandyk R, Anninos PA. 1992 Attenuation of epilepsy with application of external magnetic field: case report. Int J Neurosci 1992; 66(1-2): 75-85.

Sandyk R. 1994 Alzheimer's disease: improvement of visual memory and visuoconstructive performance treatment with picotesla range magnetic fields. Int J Neurosci 1994a; 76(3-4): 185-225.

Sandyk R. 1994 A drug-naïve Parkinsonian patient successfully treated with weak electromagnetic fields. Int J Neurosci 1994b; 79(1-2): 99.

Sisken B.F., Walker J., and Orgel M. 1993 Prospects on clinical applications of electrical stimulation for nerve regeneration. J. Cell Biochem. 51, 404-409.

Trock DH. 1994 The effect of pulsed electromagnetic fields in the